FOTHERINGHAM'S

Extraordinary Sporting Pastimes

First published in Great Britain in 2006 by
Robson Books
151 Freston Road
London
W10 6TH

An imprint of Anova Books Company Ltd

ISBN 1 86105 953 1

10 9 8 7 6 5 4 3 2 1

Illustrations by Gary Weston

Jacket artwork by Gary Weston
Jacket cover by Nichola Smith

Printed and bound by MPG Books Ltd, Bodmin, Cornwall.

This book can be ordered direct from the publisher
Contact the marketing department, but try your bookshop first

www.anovabooks.com

FOTHERINGHAM'S
Extraordinary Sporting Pastimes

William Fotheringham

ROBSON
BOOKS

HF	HS	HO	
12/06	6/07	12/07	

Acknowledgements

This book could not have been written without the contribution of Nick Brownlee, whose hard work and tireless research made the whole thing possible; thanks are also due to Gary Weston for the illustrations. I also owe a considerable debt to Malcolm Croft and Ian Allen, for steering the book seamlessly through the various stages of production, and to Helen Ponting, for handling publicity.

I should also thank my sports editor at the *Guardian*, Ben Clissitt, for his continuing support. As ever, though, Caroline, Patrick and Miranda deserve the real plaudits for their patience and understanding as one book follows another.

About the Author

William Fotheringham writes chiefly on cycle racing and rugby for the *Guardian* and *Observer*. A former racing cyclist, he has edited specialist cycling magazines and written three books on the sport, including a highly successful biography of Tom Simpson, the British cyclist who died during the Tour de France in the 1960s. Called *Put Me Back On My Bike* (Yellow Jersey), it has been hailed as 'the best cycling biography ever written'. He was also the editor/compiler of *Fotheringham's Sporting Trivia*.

Preface

In researching *Fotheringham's Sporting Trivia* in 2003, three things rapidly became clear. Firstly, Trivia might be something of a misnomer where sport is concerned. It was not so much a matter of what Bill Shankly saw about life and death being less 'important' than soccer as an awareness that even though sport was made of lots of small individual parts, those parts were not exactly trivia. Pretty much every one of them mattered to someone, somewhere, somehow.

Secondly, it was blindingly obvious that the nether reaches of sport were vast and relatively uncharted. At the time, I compared it to the Total Perspective Vortex of Douglas Adams' *Hitch-Hiker's Guide to the Galaxy* experience, but another parallel was achieved when looking at Australia: you have a general awareness that it's there and it's big, but the sheer scale of it does not hit you until you start flying across it. There was a hell of a lot going on out there beyond the few 'major' sports that are afforded serious attention by the broadsheet newspapers for whom I work.

There are two ways of dealing with this, assuming you believe – as I did and still do – that what Kazakhs get up to on horseback and what exactly is or are craps, matters as much as what snooker players have which nickname or precisely what and where is a metatarsal.

You could, if so minded and sufficiently determined, attempt to put your own shape on the entire sporting universe, to structure it and make it coherent for everyone to understand. That way, I suspect, lies madness or at least a lifetime's seclusion and a very big book. You only have to think of Proust. And then move on rapidly. Sport, after all, is supposed to be about fun, not mapping.

The alternative is to prompt people to go out and look for themselves, in the hope that they will go and explore further. To do that, one has to skim the teeming ocean of information, pop in the fishing net and see what comes up. If you have an inquisitive mind and delight in the strange and wonderful things that people do, you will rarely be disappointed.

The other question was an old one that has prompted drunken conversations in pubs and discussions in the IOC: what constitutes a sport? Where do the barriers lie between a sport and a hobby? If tiddlywinks is acceptable as a competitive endeavour, what about wood chopping? If you laugh at the notion that the latter might be a sport, take a trip to the Basque Country, where they whack axes into logs with extreme prejudice on a daily basis, or ponder the worth of bunging a spear or doing dressage.

The only answer is that the location of the barrier lies in the mind of the individual participant and the individual observer: everyone will have their own idea of where it lies; cynics might say that, at the highest level, the marketing men and television executives have rather more say in setting the barriers than perhaps they ought.

Hence, this book goes further than my first foray into that grey zone where soccer meets skydiving and cricket rubs shoulders with bog snorkelling.

Enjoy the trip.

William Fotheringham

FOTHERINGHAM'S
Extraordinary Sporting Pastimes

THE SPORTSMAN'S PRAYER

'Oh God, please bless Mum and Dad and keep me safe in the night, and oh God, please make me a sportsman.'
– Hugh de Selincourt, *The Cricket Match,* (1924)

STAIR CLIMBING

Most of us are out of puff just getting to the first landing. But Marek Schuster of Germany climbed up and down 93,932 stairs within 12 hours at Augsburg town hall on 26 May 2005. This equals a vertical distance of 15km – almost twice the height of Mount Everest.

EASY AS FALLING OFF A LOG

Well, not quite. Log-rolling might seem a simple enough concept – two men at either end of a log attempting to spin each other into the water – but for the novice it is devilishly hard to master. Competitors wear spiked boots and aim for the best of three falls. To be good requires anticipation, speed of thought, balance, and a tap-dancer's twinkle toes. In 1900, it is reported that one match lasted nearly three hours!

DEAD F1 DRIVERS

Despite speeds in excess of 200mph, Formula One is today one of the safest sports there is thanks to the efforts of its governing body, in conjunction with manufacturers and drivers. It was not always so, unfortunately, as this grim roll call of fatalities proves:

ONOFRE MARIMON	(Mase), Nurburgring, Germany, 1954, (practice)
PETER COLLINS	(Ferrari), Nurburgring, Germany, 1958
STEWART LEWIS-EVANS	(Vanwall), Ain-Diab, Morocco, 1958
CHRIS BRISTOW	(Coop), Spa, Belgium, 1960
WOLFGANG von TRIPS	(Ferrari), Monza, Italy, 1961
RICARDO RODRIGUEZ	(Lotus), Autodromo Hermanos Rodriguez, Mexico, 1962
LORENZO BANDINI	(Ferrari), Monaco, 1967
JIM CLARK	(Lotus), Hockenheim, Germany, 1968
PIERS COURAGE	(De Tomaso), Zandvoort, Holland, 1970
JOCHEN RINDT	(Lotus), Monza, Italy, 1970 (practice)
FRANÇOIS CEVERT	(Tyrrell), Watkin's Glen, USA, 1973
PETER REVSON	(Ford), Johannesburg, South Africa, 1974 (practice)
MARK DONOHUE	(March), Osterreichring, Austria, 1975 (practice)
TOM PRYCE	(Shadow), Kyalami, South Africa, 1977
RONNIE PETERSON	(Lotus), Monza, Italy, 1978
PATRICK DEPAILLER	(Alfa Romeo), Hockenheim, Germany, 1980 (practice)
RICCARDO PALETTI	(Osella), Ile Notre-Dame, Canada, 1982
GILLES VILLENEUVE	(Ferrari), Spa, Belgium, 1982
ROLAND RATZENBERGER	(Simtek), Monza, Italy, 1994 (practice)
AYRTON SENNA	(Williams-Renault), Monza, Italy, 1994

ALL ABOARD THE GUMBALL RALLY

The Gumball Rally was a wacky 1970s movie in which a collection of souped-up vehicles raced each other across the USA. It was inspired by the real-life coast-to-coast race named the *Cannonball Baker Sea-To-Shining-Sea Memorial Trophy Dash* – itself inspired by the exploits of legendary motorcyclist 'Cannonball' Baker, who first achieved the feat in 1933.

The race was scrapped in 1979, but 20 years later 'Gumball 3000' was launched. This was a six-day, 3,000-mile trek around Europe featuring celebrities like Kate Moss, Guy Ritchie, Billy Zane and Monica Lewinsky. Like the movie, competitors not only raced each other but enjoyed nightly parties and stopovers at luxury hotels. The event proved such a success that it has been repeated every year since. In 2006, the race consisted of 120 vehicles and 240 competitors and the aim was to drive around the world in just eight days. The entrance fee was a cool £40,000.

PERKAIN – KING OF PELOTA

Pelota is a handball-style game played on a long court with a hard ball and a curved bat that resembles a bicycle mudguard. Few people outside Basque Spain will have heard of the sport, and even fewer will have heard of Perkain, its greatest ever player. Even today, nearly 200 years after his death, Perkain's prowess on the pelota court continues to be celebrated in his native country. A favourite is the story of his marathon three-hour game against his great rival Ezkerra. Having won the match, Perkain returned to his village to find the local police waiting to arrest him for some unspecified misdemeanour. With what can only be described as the most accurate shot of the day, Perkain threw the ball 50 yards at the police chief's head, knocking him out and allowing him to make a daring escape.

AMATEUR GOLF – THE DANGERS

Golf is, of course, a hugely popular sporting pastime and provides pleasure for millions of amateur hackers. It is not without its hazards, however. In 1963, 24-handicapper Jim Armstrong teed off at the Desert Forest Golf Club in Carefree, Arizona. His shot hit the tee marker and ricocheted back into his face, briefly knocking him senseless. When he recovered his wits sufficiently to tee off again, his second ball hit the same post, ricocheted back again and broke his left kneecap.

THE MEXICAN WAVE

Despite its name, it's thought the Mexican wave – in which the crowd create a ripple effect around the stadium by standing up and sitting down again in unison – originated across the border in the USA. Specifically, the first wave is thought to have taken place at the home of the Oakland Athletics baseball team in 1981, where professional cheerleader 'Krazy' George Henderson dreamt it up.

However, there is no doubt that it became a global phenomenon at the 1986 football World Cup finals in Mexico, where the vast human waves were often far more entertaining than some of the drab football on offer. Since then it has become a standard side-attraction at all major sporting events. Indeed, the largest ever-recorded wave was at the Sydney Olympics in 2000, when a crowd in excess of 110,000 made an inverse Mexican wave and two simultaneous opposite direction waves.

SUNDAY LEAGUE FOOTBALL

Conservative estimates suggest there are around 10,000 Sunday League teams in England alone, many affiliated to the local pub. What is certain is that every Sunday morning in the winter, regardless of the weather or how much alcohol has been consumed the night before, thousands of amateur footballers turn up at their local park for a kick-around. While most players are confirmed amateurs, Sunday League has produced several top stars, including former Arsenal striker Ian Wright who was spotted scoring goals for a side called Ten Em Bees on Hackney Marshes.

However, the gulf between Sunday League and professional is football vast, as Oxbarn Social Club from Wolverhampton discovered in 1973 during a tour to Germany.

SUNDAY LEAGUE FOOTBALL (CONTINUED . . .)

Arrangements had been made to play a local side, but when Oxbarn turned up they discovered their opponents were Bundesliga outfit SVW Mainz, who themselves were expecting to play Wolverhampton Wanderers. The match went ahead anyway, with the Germans running out 21–0 winners. Oxbarn, however, easily won the rematch in the bar afterwards.

OFFICE OLYMPICS

Increasingly popular among bored young workers, Office Olympics utilises office furniture and layout to create a series of competitive events. These include:

- Office Chair Swamp: competitors wade through a 'swamp' of spring-loaded office swivel chairs, with the person getting the best time from one side to the other being declared the winner.
- Cubicle Hurdles: here competitors race from one side of the office to the other, using plywood cubicle partitions as hurdles.
- Chair-iot Racing: a head-to-head corridor race between two competitors on office chairs.
- Trash Can Long Jump: competitors are given a short run-up, then must leap an increasingly long line of metal waste-paper bins.
- Office Chair Battles: a form of 21st century jousting, in which competitors attempt to dismount their opponent by crashing into them.
- Corridor Sprinting: a straight foot-race between two competitors along a corridor. This event has been out of favour ever since two New York lawyers raced each other for money, resulting in one smashing through a plate-glass window and plunging 39 floors to his death.

JOGGING FIXX

In 1979 runner Jay Helgerson ran a marathon every week of the year – except for one, when he got bored and ran two in one weekend. He was perhaps the most extreme example of the jogging boom that swept the USA in the late 1970s and that has become a standard form of exercise for millions of people ever since. The craze is generally attributed to Jim Fixx, a reformed overweight smoker whose 1977 manual *The Complete Book of Running* became an instant bestseller. In 1984 Fixx famously dropped dead of a heart attack, but while this was a cause of great celebration among couch potatoes it did little to deter advocates of the pastime. The popularity of charity fun runs and huge-scale events such as the London Marathon has never been greater.

FAMOUS BOXERS

Boxing may not be the sport of kings, but it is certainly the pastime of celebrities if this list of famous pugilists is anything to go by:

Norman Wisdom (comedian, 1932 Army boxing champion)
Teddy Roosevelt (US President)
Lord Byron (poet)
Berry Gordy (founder of Motown Records)
George Stephenson (inventor of the steam locomotive)
Pope John Paul II
Eamonn Andrews (presenter of *This Is Your Life*)
Kris Kristofferson (actor and singer)
Terence Trent D'Arby (singer)
Idi Amin (dictator, Ugandan heavyweight champion for nine years)
Bob Hope (comedian)
Arthur Mullard (comedian)
Billy Joel (singer)
Chris Isaak (singer)
John Fashanu (footballer)
Jack Palance (actor)
Ernest Hemingway (novelist)

LUDUS DUODECIM SCRIPTORUM

Back in the first century BC, more than two thousand years before online poker, every trendy Roman was playing Ludus Duodecim Scriptorum. Indeed the distinctive gameboards – consisting of rows of engraved hearts, stars and semi-circles – have been found throughout the Roman Empire, and it is mentioned specifically in Ovid's seminal work *Ars Amatoria*. Unfortunately, no one has ever discovered the rules. All that is known for certain is that players moved their pieces according to the throw of three dice which were, in turn, thrown into a *fritillus*, a wooden tower about ten inches high with a spiral staircase inside. The dice fell down the staircase and spilled out onto the playing surface through a small exit. The idea of this, it is thought, was to prevent accusations of cheating which could and often did result in punch-ups and even murder.

Ludus Duodecim Scriptorum gradually fell out of favour in the first century AD and was replaced by Tabula, a game that would eventually mutate into Backgammon.

SPORT CRAZY

The English actor Trevor Howard was such an avid cricket fan that he had a clause in all his movie contracts stating that he would not be required for filming during any Test match played at Lord's. Meanwhile comedian-turned-actor Alan Davies refuses to turn up to filming whenever his beloved Arsenal are playing at home.

BEER-MAT FLIPPING

Beer-mat flipping is perhaps the archetypal pub sport, involving virtually no physical exercise other than using one hand to flip and catch as many beer mats as possible from off the edge of the table. Inevitably there are those who take it more seriously than others, in this case Felixstowe flipper Dean Gould, who holds virtually every beer-mat flipping world record. These include:

- Simultaneous (two hands) flipping: 130 (65 caught in each hand), January 1987
- Speed flipping: 1,000 mats flipped in 45 seconds (25 piles of 40), October 1993

Gould also holds the record for the greatest number of 10p-piece snatching, when in January 1993 he caught 328.

IT'S A RECORD BREAKER

World records are usually associated with 'legitimate' sports such as athletics. However, it seems that the Olympic ideal of *Citius, Altius, Fortius* (Swifter, Higher, Stronger) can be applied to just about any pastime – as this oddball collection from the *Guinness Book of World Records* demonstrates.

Domino toppling: 3,992,397 dominoes toppled in November 2004, in Leeuwarden, Netherlands by a 90-strong international team.

Simon Says: Record set by 597 participants in China in December 2004.

Human conveyor belt: In March 2005, students from Taylorsville, Utah passed a mattress along a line of 100 people in 2 minutes 1 second.

Tallest Lego tower: This was built using 500,000 Lego bricks in February 2005 at Legoland, California. It measured a height of 92ft 6in (28.19m)

Throwing a playing card: Rick Smith Jr, of Lyndhurst, California threw a playing card 216ft (66m) in December 2002.

Roller-coaster riding: From 10 July to 28 August 2003, Richard Rodriguez, a teacher from Chicago, rode 'Expedition Ge Force' in Haßloch, Germany non-stop. During those 49 days he covered 18,642 miles (30,000 km).

Crawling: Leo Chau and Sean Duffy crawled 32.26 miles (51.925km) around Rampart High School Football Field, Colorado in May 2005. It took them 45 hours 10 minutes.

Balloon stuffing: Ralf Schüler from Dessau, Germany managed to squeeze 23 people inside a latex balloon in 2002.

Beer glass balancing: In November 2003, John Evans, of Heanor, Derbyshire, balanced 235 pints of beer on his head, breaking his previously held record of 230.

Tiddlywinking: The record for completing a tiddlywink mile solo is held by Ralf Laue of Stamberg, Germany who made it in 1hr 6mins in November 2003.

Card holding: In March 1994 the multi-talented Ralf Laue held a fan of 326 playing cards in one hand the value and colour of each card was clearly visible on one side of the card, and no adhesives were used.

Train pulling: Georges Christen from Luxemburg pulled a 20.5 ton railway carriage with his teeth for a distance of 656ft (200m) in August 1985.

A TASTE OF THE ORIENT

If golf is a good walk spoiled, then what does that make the gruelling sport of orienteering? Every weekend, thousands of enthusiasts head for the wilderness armed only with a map, a compass and a pair of running shoes. Their aim? To locate and discover fiendishly concealed control points in the fastest time, thus completing the course. Perhaps not surprisingly, the sport was dreamed up by a military man. In 1918, noticing that there was a decided lack of interest in field athletics among youngsters in his native Sweden, Major Ernst Killander decided to do something about it. He gathered together a group of teenagers and drove them to the nearest forest. Equipping them with map and compass, he gave them instructions to find their way back to the starting point by means of waypoints. Whether Killander's kids ever got back is unknown. However, the sport quickly took off, and today more than sixty countries are affiliated to the International Orienteering Federation.

KITE FIGHTING

In most countries, kite flying is a relaxing pastime for all the family. In Thailand, smashing them into each other is a hugely popular competitive sport. Contests are fought with two types of specialised kites. The Pakpao is diamond-shaped with a long tail and, because it is just 2.5ft (76cm) in length it can be manoeuvred by just one person. The Chula, by contrast, is 5ft (1.5m) or more in length and shaped as a five-pointed star. Two people are needed to keep this monster in the air.

The rules of kite fighting are archaic and complex, but essentially the aim is to destroy the other kite by knocking it out of the sky. Aerial bouts can last up to an hour, and attract large crowds.

LIFEGUARD GAMES

The TV show *Baywatch* portrayed beach lifeguards as a bunch of finely honed, bronzed athletes. But it is unlikely that even David Hasselhoff would make much of an impact at the annual Lifeguard Games. First staged in 1967 in California the Games has become a highly charged international championship in which competing lifeguards battle it out over a series of events including swimming, rowing and sprinting over sand dunes.

HAWAIIAN IRONMAN

Held annually in Hawaii, the Ironman Triathlon World Championship features three endurance events: swimming, biking and running. It is based in Kailua Kona, and involves a 2.4-mile (3.86km) swim across Kailua Kona Bay, followed by a 112-mile (180.2km) bike ride and a 26.2-mile (42.2km) marathon along the coast of the Big Island. The World Championship is the blue-riband event in the Ironman calendar and attracts up to 1,800 competitors aged 18–80 from more than 50 countries. It is not for the fainthearted: the average Ironman triathlete spends 18 to 24 hours each week training for this event. A typical week includes 7 miles of swimming, 225 miles of biking and 48 miles of running.

THOSE MAGNIFICENT MEN...

If you've never seen a 6ft toilet fly through the air then the chances are you've never been to a Flugtag. A uniquely loony competition, Flugtag (the word is German for 'flying day') involves manpowered flying machines launched from a 6m high ramp into the sea below. Once the preserve of a few hardcore eccentrics, the sport now boasts high-profile sponsorship and international competition.

In the USA more than 200 teams take part, and the event is televised live. The British version takes place every year at the Firth of Forth, and flying machines have included a trailer home, a giant taco, and even a flying fish. Competitors are judged on the distance of their flight, the creativity of their machine and their pre-flight performance.

Such high-octane competition needs rules, of course – and the main restrictions are as follows:

- All flying machines must be launched from the 6m high runway, using only human power
- No auxiliary lifting devices, power sources, or stored energy (e.g. elastic, batteries, clockwork springs, rocket fuel etc.) may be used
- Modified aircraft – e.g. paragliders, hang-gliders, jet-fighter planes, light aircraft, commercial jets etc. – are not permitted
- For their own safety, competitors must be able to swim a minimum of 100m unaided

SURFING OBSESSION

'It is a remarkable fact that once tried, surfing becomes an obsession, and the more one becomes involved with it, so it becomes a philosophy – a way of life.'
– Carl Thomson, *Surfing in Great Britain*

WISH YOU WERE HERE?

While most of us go on holiday to relax, the ideal vacation for an Extreme Tourist is one in which death is a distinct possibility. Essentially, extreme tourism involves travelling to dangerous places, such as mountains, jungles, deserts and caves. Indeed it has proved a booming business in parts of the world not normally associated with tourism of any kind. Top of the list are the former Soviet states, including Russia, Ukraine and Armenia, where it is possible to fly in a MiG fighter jet at Mach 2.5, go ice diving in the White Sea, or even travel across the Chernobyl zone. All that is required is a passport and a couple of thousand pounds. Needless to say, it is virtually impossible to sign up for life insurance.

A LEAP INTO THE UNKNOWN

Why spend a fortune on hiring a plane when there are any number of tall bridges and buildings to fling yourself from? That is the simple theory behind the sport of BASE jumping, in which people leap from fixed objects with only a parachute to save them. 'BASE' stands for the four categories of objects from which one can jump: Building, Antenna (an uninhabited tower such as an aerial mast), Span (a bridge, arch or dome), and Earth (a cliff or other natural formation). Although it is regarded as a modern phenomenon, the earliest recorded BASE jump was in 1912 when Frederick Law leaped from the Statue of Liberty in New York. The sport was popularised and given its name in 1978 when film-maker Carl Boenish recorded himself jumping from the 3,000ft El Capitan cliff in Yosemite National Park. For several years Boenish was the pre-eminent BASE jumper, and his dramatic films captured the imagination of a new generation of jumpers. Sadly he would also highlight the inherent dangers of the sport when he was killed on a cliff jump in Norway.

BODYBOARDING

Hardcore surfers may scoff, but bodyboarding has become a hugely popular sport in recent years – and many of its top exponents claim it is even harder to master than traditional surfing.

The main piece of kit required is a small, rectangular piece of hardened foam shaped to a hydrodynamic form. While the bodyboard is ridden predominantly lying down (or 'prone'), making it accessible to most amateurs, experts have mastered the half-standing stance (known as 'dropknee') or even standing up. Championships are held wherever there are waves, although the main centre of popularity remains the west coast of America.

CREASED UP

There are few pastimes that can be said to combine high-energy sport with housework – but then there is something quite unique about the sport of Extreme Ironing (EI). Essentially, EI involves doing the ironing at extreme locations, such as mountaintops, underwater, halfway down ski slopes and even 2,000ft in the air. The ironing itself has variations: either solo or in a group; ironing in existing formations or freestyle.

The concept was dreamed up in 1999 by enthusiast Phil Shaw, from Leicester, who claims it 'combines the thrill of an extreme sport with the satisfaction of a well-pressed shirt.'

Since then, his oddball hobby has become a huge phenomenon, with clubs and enthusiasts all over the world. In September 2002, the first world championship for the sport took place in Germany, with competitors from Austria, Australia, Croatia, Chile, Germany and the UK.

Since the sport's invention, there has been the formation of an alleged breakaway group, Urban Housework – taking a vacuum cleaner and tidying up the outdoors for the good of humanity.

PIG-STICKING

Animal-rights enthusiasts will take no comfort at all from the fact that pig-sticking came into existence, as a substitute for bear sticking once the bears, not unsurprisingly, became scarce. Nor will they be particularly enamoured by the rules of this arcane but once highly enjoyed colonial pastime.

Three riders, armed with spears, wait while local beaters drive wild boars from the undergrowth. Once the boar is sighted, a mad melee ensues in which the first rider to drive his spear through the unfortunate porker is the winner.

In his seminal work on the subject, *Pig-sticking or Hog-hunting: A Complete Account for Sportsmen – And Others*, Sir Robert Baden-Powell gives the following terms for a pig:

Soot

Bad

Dukar

Paddi

Kard

Hundi

Cunijati

Banda

Baden-Powell – who between the years 1882–84 claimed to have bagged 428 pigs – also describes the pastime thus: 'Perhaps, excepting murder pig-sticking is one of the oldest sports in the world.'

NORBERT DENTRESSANGLING

For years, Eddie Stobart-spotters have gathered on motorway bridges for a glimpse of the Cumbrian-based haulage firm's distinctive lorries. But a breakaway group of Euro-trucking enthusiasts have now switched their attention to wagons belonging to Stobart's French rival Norbert Dentressangle. Bryan Wiley, of 'Dentressanglers UK', says: 'They come from all over the continent and it's a thrill to compare notes with other spotters to see where they've been. The attraction is in the smart livery – and, of course, the unmistakeable name.'

SOME FAMOUS QUOTES ON HUNTING

'There is a passion for hunting something deeply implanted in the human breast'
–Charles Dickens

'When you have shot one bird flying you have shot all birds flying. They are all different and they fly in different ways but the sensation is the same and the last one is as good as the first.'
–Ernest Hemingway

'It is very strange, and very melancholy, that the paucity of human pleasures should persuade us ever to call hunting one of them.'
–Samuel Johnson

'When a man wants to murder a tiger he calls it sport; when a tiger wants to murder him he calls it ferocity.'
–George Bernard Shaw

'One knows so well the popular idea of health. The English country gentleman galloping after a fox – the unspeakable in full pursuit of the uneatable.'
–Oscar Wilde

DENIS COMPTON

Thanks to the rise and rise of professionalism, Denis Compton will probably be the last sportsman to play professional football for a top side and cricket for England.

And, long before David Beckham, Compton was used to promote Brylcreem.

He scored his first Test century as a precocious 19-year-old in 1938 against Don Bradman's touring Australians. He finished his cricket career after playing 78 Test matches with 17 centuries at an average of 50.06. In all first-class cricket he scored 123 centuries.

Compton spent his entire football career at Arsenal. A winger, he made his debut in 1936, and won the League in 1948 and the FA Cup in 1950. However, the latter part of his sporting career was dogged by knee trouble, which limited him to 60 official (i.e. non-wartime) appearances and 16 goals. He represented England in wartime 12 times, but never in a full official match. He died in 1991 at the age of 73.

PAST PRESIDENTS OF THE LORD'S TAVERNERS

Since 1950, cricket charity the Lord's Taverners has raised millions of pounds for deserving causes. Its membership is a roll call of celebrities past and present, as this list of its Presidents indicates:

Sir John Mills, actor, 1950–51
John Snagge, commentator, 1952 and 1964
Martin Boddey, actor, 1953 and 1971
Jack Hawkins, actor, 1954
Major A Huskisson, soldier, 1955
Tommy Trinder, comedian, 1956
Stephen Mitchell, theatrical impresario, 1957
Sir John Barbirolli, conductor, 1958
Sir Ian Jacob, Chairman of the BBC Board of Governors, 1959
HRH The Duke of Edinburgh, 1960–61
The Rt Hon. Sir Robert Menzies, Australian prime minister, 1962
Richard Hearne, actor, 1963
Sir Edward Lewis, owner of Decca records, 1965
Ronnie Waldman, BBC Head of Light Entertainment, 1966
Sir Harry Secombe, comedian, 1967–68 and 1980–81
The Rt Hon. Lord Luke of Pavenham, 1969
Brian Rix, actor and fundraiser, 1970
Victor Silvester, dancer, 1972
Jimmy Edwards, comedian, 1973
Alf Gover, England cricketer, 1974
HRH The Prince of Wales, 1975–76
Eric Morecambe OBE, comedian, 1977–79
Ronnie Corbett, comedian, 1982 and 1987
Terry Wogan, broadcaster, 1983–84
David Frost, broadcaster, 1985–86
Sir Tim Rice, lyricist, 1988–90 and 2000
Leslie Crowther, comedian, 1991–92
HRH Prince Edward, 1993–94
The Lord Cowdrey of Tonbridge (Colin Cowdrey), cricketer, 1995–97
Nicholas Parsons, broadcaster, 1998–99
Robert Powell, actor, 2001–02
Richard Stilgoe, comedian, 2003–2004
Mike Gatting, cricketer 2004–

THE EARLY DAYS OF THE GRAND NATIONAL

- In 1839, seventeen horses and their riders lined up at Aintree for a race of 'four miles across country' – the Grand Liverpool Steeplechase. The event drew a crowd of 40,000 spectators.

- The rules for the first National were: 'A sweepstake of 20 sovereigns each, five sovereigns forfeit, with 100 sovereigns added; 12 stone each; gentlemen riders; four miles across country; the second horse to save his stake, and the winner to pay ten sovereigns towards expenses; no rider to open a gate or ride through a gateway, or more than 100 yards along any road, path or driftway'.

- The first National was due to start at 1 p.m. but eventually got underway at 3 p.m. after confusion in the weighing-out procedure and a succession of false starts. The eventual winner was the aptly named Lottery, the 5–1 favourite.

- Becher's Brook was named after Captain Martin Becher, one of the country's top jockeys. In the first ever race his horse ploughed into the sixth fence and catapulted Becher over the top and into the brook.

- After the first National was run, the *Liverpool Mercury* newspaper bemoaned: 'We have heard with alarm and regret that it is in contemplation to establish steeplechasing annually or periodically in this neighbourhood. If any such design is seriously entertained we trust that some means will be adopted to defeat it!'

- Tom Olliver was the first jockey to win back to back Nationals, riding Gay Lad in 1842 and Vanguard the following year, the first time the race was run as a handicap. He was so pleased with Vanguard that he had a sofa made from the bay gelding's hide when the horse died. Olliver took part in a record eighteen Nationals despite a spell behind bars in a debtor's prison, boasting three wins, three seconds and a third.

- In 1862 James Wynne was due to ride O'Connell in the National, but on the morning of the race he learned that his sister had died suddenly at home in Ireland. O'Connell's owner, Lord De Freyne, tried to persuade Wynne not to ride, but he was determined to take part to honour his sister. During the race, O'Connell fell and Wynne suffered internal injuries from which he died that evening.

PUNTING PARLANCE

You might well lose your shirt betting on the horses, but this guide to the arcane and often baffling lingo of the turf will at least help you understand why you lost:

AGE: Worked out from 1 January each year, regardless of a horse's real birthday

AGED: Over six years old

AIRING: Horse in a race for the exercise, not the money

AMISS: Filly or mare 'in season' – naturally tending to run below par

ANTE-POST: Betting before the day of the race – odds are normally better, but you lose on non-runners

BUMPER: Amateur rider

CHALK JOCKEY: Rider not experienced enough to have his name printed in permanent letters on the number board

DOG: Non-trier

GENUINE: A trier

MAIDEN: A horse that hasn't won yet

MONKEY: £500

NURSERY: Handicap for two-year-olds only

OUT OF: A horse's parents

PONY: £25

STAYER: A horse that comes into its own after a mile-and-a-half or more

TRIPLE CROWN: The Derby, 2000 Guineas and the St Leger

IN A FLAP

Although it is traditionally associated with flat caps and northern towns, pigeon racing is a major sport played for high stakes and even higher reputations. Competitions may vary in importance, but the fundamentals of the sport are easy to grasp. Pigeons are removed by an agreed distance from their home coops and then released at a predetermined time. The arrival of each bird at its home coop is carefully recorded. For each bird, a velocity, usually in metres per minute or yards per minute, is calculated from the recorded time and the distance the coop is from the release point. The winner is the bird with the greatest velocity.

Speed, of course, is a major advantage to a champion pigeon, but so is 'homing' ability and stamina. Flights as long as 1,689 miles have been recorded by exceptional birds in competition.

ELEPHANT RACING

In June 2000, despite protests by animal rights activists, more than 40,000 people crammed into Berlin's Hoppegarten to watch Europe's first elephant race. Fourteen circus elephants, half African and half Asian and each of them ridden by a jockey, battled it out over a 300m course to claim the top prize – extra helpings of fruit and vegetables.

INVENTED SPORTS

While there are literally hundreds of perfectly adequate traditional sports to take up, some folk are never satisfied unless they've got their own. Here is a rundown of some invented sports that have somehow become popular.

Chess boxing: Invented in 1922, chess boxing is a contest between two opponents consisting of up to eleven alternating rounds of boxing and chess, starting with a four-minute chess round followed by two minutes of boxing and so on. Between rounds there is a one-minute pause, during which competitors change their kit.

Crockey: Two teams of one to three players propel a ball back and forth using hands, feet and a bat. A team scores a point by getting the ball to stop on the opposing team's side.

Danball: A street-based game in which players attempt to advance a ball, hitting it with implements called Dansticks, across one of two goal lines to score points.

Disc Golf (AKA **folf, frolf** or **frisbee golf**): Based loosely on the rules of golf, flying discs are thrown towards a target, which serves as the 'hole'. The targets can range from objects, such as trees and poles, to metal baskets with hanging chains to catch the discs.

Ringo: Popular in Poland, this sport is played on a rectangular court with a raised net, similar to volleyball or badminton. Individual players or teams stand on opposite sides of the net and throw a small rubber ring back and forth, without letting it hit the ground.

It was invented by Wlodzimierz Strzyzewski, a Polish fencer and journalist, who demonstrated the game while he was covering the 1968 Olympics in Mexico City.

Scuffleball: A combination of American football and rugby, played by two teams of twelve players. Players advance the ball by running, passing or tossing it to team-mates in an attempt to out manoeuvre the opposition into the end zone. Play is free-flowing and relatively stoppage free.

ETAPE DU TOUR

Every year around 8,000 cycle nuts get to fulfil their dream and ride a stage of the Tour de France. The Etape du Tour (literally, Stage of the Tour) takes place on a section of the route on which the professional peloton will ride a couple of days later. It is authentic right down to the motorcycle outriders, the support cars and the crowds lining the route in their thousands. The gradients are all too authentic as well; in 2006, the route took in the 2360m Col D'Izoard, the 2058m Col de Lautaret, and the infamous 21 hairpins of the Alpe D'Huez.

HOW TO LAUNCH A HOT-AIR BALLOON

A typical hot-air balloon flight starts with unpacking the balloon from its carrying bag. A petrol powered fan is used to blow cold air into the envelope. This partially inflates the balloon to establish its basic shape before the burner flame is aimed into the throat, heating the air inside. A crew member stationed opposite the throat, holds a rope tied to the apex (crown) of the envelope. The 'crown-man' acts as a dead weight in order to slow the envelope's rise so that the envelope can achieve maximum inflation before standing erect. Once the balloon is upright, pilot and passengers climb into the basket. When the pilot is ready for launch, more heat is directed into the envelope and the balloon lifts off gradually.

HENLEY REGATTA

The Henley Regatta was first held in 1839, when it was staged by the mayor of Henley as a public attraction with a fair and other amusements. It proved so popular that it has been staged annually ever since, but with the emphasis changed so that competitive amateur rowing has become its main purpose.

In 1886 the Regatta was extended to three days, then four in 1906 and five in 1986. Since 1928 its increased popularity meant entries exceeded the permitted numbers in several events, and so qualifying races are now held in the week before the Regatta to reduce the number of entries to the permitted maximum.

AN A–Z of LESSER-KNOWN FOREIGN CARD GAMES

Alcalde (Spain): played with a pack of 40 cards, the aim is to take as many tricks as possible.

Calabresella (Italy): a point-trick game for three players involving bidding and tactics.

Durak (Russia): 'Durak' is Russian for 'fool' – which describes the player who is left with the most cards at the end of this throwing-in game.

Encaje (Basque Spain): a series of 'hot' cards are passed between the players with the aim of getting rid of them.

French Tarot (France): played with a special pack of 78 cards, this is a complex bidding game.

Gong Zhu (China): a Chinese version of 'Hearts', translated as 'Hunt The Pig'.

Hanafuda (Japan): the object is to capture scoring cards from a 48-card pack.

Illusztrált tarokk (Hungary): players must attempt to outbid each other – the loser is traditionally obliged to wear a silly hat.

Kalter Schlag (Germany): a trick-taking game in which the loser is the first to accumulate 2,000 points.

Laugavatnsmanni (Iceland): players use a traditional pack, minus the twos, in this trick-taking game.

Marjapussi (Finland): similar to rummy except all cards between two and six are removed from the pack.

Nos (Netherlands): a trick-taking game in which dominoes are used to keep score.

Okey (Turkey): wooden tiles are used in this rummy-style game instead of traditional cards.

Phat (Scotland): ancient Celtic game also known as nine-card Dom.

Quitlok (Transylvania): a game played for money with special cards originally devised to avoid religious bans on card games.

Umtali (Zimbabwe): a rummy game for two people said to have originated on rail journeys in colonial Rhodesia.

Viet Cong (Vietnam): the aim is to get rid of your cards by beating the combinations of your opponents.

Yablon (Mexico): banking game in which players must bet on the turn of a card.

OCTOPUSH

In 1954 four divers from Southsea, Hants – John Ventham, Alan Blake, Jack Willis and Frank Lilleker – decided to show the versatility of their scuba tanks by playing a game of hockey underwater in the local swimming pool. The game was picked up by other divers and, with a strange inevitability, the sport of Octopush was born. The sport is similar to ice hockey, with two teams attempting to manoeuvre a puck by sliding it across the bottom of the pool into the opponent's goal. It remains a minority sport, largely due to lack of spectators.

LAWNMOWER RACING.

Who needs expensive Formula One cars? In 1973, a group of motor-sport fans from a pub in Wisborough Green, West Sussex, decided to try their hand at racing souped-up mowers. The craze took off, and now thousands of enthusiasts turn up every year with their jet-powered lawnmowers to events such as the World Championship, the British Grand Prix and the annual twelve-hour endurance race.

All organised sport needs rules and classifications – and lawnmower racing is no different:

Class 1 – These are walk-behind lawnmowers which travel as fast as whoever is pushing them.

Class 2 – Roller-driven mowers with a towed seat. Typically these machines would cut cricket pitches and bowling greens and are capable of speeds up to 35mph.

Class 3 – Small garden mowers powered by a 10hp engine. These are capable of speeds in excess of 50mph and are the favoured class among competitors.

Class 4 – A new class for small bonneted tractors. These machines are regarded as the future of the sport as they boast potential top speeds of over 50mph.

CATAPULTING

Not the sort of catty that Dennis the Menace used to break windows with, but the huge wooden sort once used in medieval sieges. Enthusiasts stage regular competitions to see whose home-made catapult can fling them the furthest distance. The sport is not without danger, however. In 2000, Stella Young from London was catapulted at more than 50mph into a net 100 yards away, and fractured her pelvis when she bounced out.

SPAMALOT

Presumably invented to kill time between meals, Spam carving has become a hugely popular pastime in the USA. Enthusiasts spend hours creating ornate sculptures from tins of processed meat, using knives, chisels and planes. At the annual world championship held in Seattle, dozens compete for the title of Spam King – and the honour of being presented with a crown made of freshly carved Spam.

WISH YOU WILL BE HERE?

Bored with run-of-the-mill tourist magnets like the Pyramids or Buckingham Palace, increasing numbers of people are now beating the crowds in order to visit sites that will be attractions in the FUTURE. Last year more than 10,000 people visited the town of Riverside, Iowa where according to *Star Trek* legend, James T Kirk, captain of the *Starship Enterprise*, will be born on 21 March, 2228.

VOLCANO BAGGING

When Mount Etna erupted in spectacular style in 2004, it was the signal for hundreds of volcano-baggers to head for Sicily, armed with cameras, notebooks, and lava-proof anoraks. Enthusiasts like to be photographed as close to the mouth of the volcano as possible, and the aim is to 'bag' every live volcano in the world for their albums. It is not without its dangers, however. In 1980, several 'baggers' were killed when Mt St Helens exploded in the USA.

BURIED ALIVE

Some folk just like to get away from it all – by burying themselves six feet underground. Self-burying is a solitary hobby, but popular nonetheless. In 1999, loner Geoff Smith of Mansfield, Notts, spent 147 days buried in a specially constructed coffin in his garden. In the process he won the world record title once held by his late mother Emma, who in 1968 spent 100 days down a hole in Skegness, Lincs.

HERE IS THE NUDES

According to the organisation British Naturism, letting it all hang out is a 'friendly, relaxing and enjoyable way to spend your free time'. And with more than 25,000 registered naturists in the UK and over two million worldwide, it's a pastime that is catching on. The number of nudist beaches is increasing all the time, too – currently there are nine on the south coast of England alone.

A SELECTION OF WRESTLING HOLDS

Anaconda vice: In a seated position the wrestler's right arm goes around the left side of his opponent's head and grabs his right wrist, bending the arm upwards. He then pulls the opponent forward, causing pressure on the opponent's arm and neck.

Camel clutch: The wrestler sits on the back of his opponent, who is face down on the mat, and reaches under his opponent's arms to apply a chinlock.

Chickenwing over the shoulder crossface: The wrestler goes to a fallen opponent and places one arm over his nearest shoulder before locking his hands around the opponent's chin.

Stretch Plum: An inverted facelock, followed by a knee in the back. The wrestler places his far leg between his opponent's legs and pushes his near leg's knee against the opponent's back.

Tongan death grip: The wrestler puts his hand under his opponent's chin, then squeezes on the pressure point above the throat.

Gutwrench: The wrestler stands behind his opponent and locks his hands around the opponent's stomach, pulling up and squeezing it.

Haas of Pain: A modified inverted reverse figure-four leglock variation developed by wrestling brothers Charlie and Russ Haas.

Gorilla press: The wrestler lifts his opponent up over his head with arms fully extended, then drops him onto the floor.

Lady of the Lake: The wrestler rolls into a ball and offers his hand between his legs. When his opponent takes it, the wrestler rolls forward, putting him in an armlock.

Pumphandle: While his opponent is bent over, the wrestler grabs his hands between his legs, lifts him up and then slams him down again.

Scoop: The opponent is lifted horizontally, then smashed to the floor.

Tilt-a-whirl: The opponent is bent over, the wrestler grabs his hands between his legs and flips him into the air.

Wheelbarrow: The wrestler wraps his opponents legs around his waist, then lifts him up with a Gutwrench manoeuvre.

Airplane spin: A spinning fireman's lift, designed to make the opponent dizzy.

Tree of woe: The opponent is suspended upside down from a corner post.

NOODLING

Fishing traditionally – and somewhat sensibily – involves the use of a rod and a line. However, in certain southern states of the USA (Lousiana, Oklahoma for example), a bizarrely-popular pastime is 'noodling' – the practice of fishing for catfish using only one's bare hands. In the UK it is known as trout-tickling, and guddling in Scotland.

DISCONTINUED OLYMPIC SPORTS

SWIMMING OBSTACLE RACE: Discontinued after 1900, this event was held over 200m, and competitors were required to climb over a pole, scramble over a row of boats, and then swim under another row of boats. Frederick Lane of Australia won gold with a time of 2 minutes 34 seconds.

JEU DE PAUM: Known in Britain as 'real tennis' or 'court tennis', this sport – dating back to the sixteenth century – was an Olympic speciality until 1908, when Jay Gould of the USA was awarded gold.

RINGING THE BULL

Ringing the Bull, like many English pub games, dates back to the Middle Ages. The idea is to swing a metal or plastic ring on a string across the room at a hook embedded in the wall. Players take turns and the person with the most 'ringers' wins. Originally, the game was played with a bull's nose ring and a bull's horn – and occasionally the whole bull's head – for a target.

BUILDERING

Buildering (also known as urban climbing, structuring or stegophily) is the highly dangerous sport of climbing the outside of tall buildings – the taller the better, and usually without any form of harnessing and certainly no safety net. Unsurprisingly, it is illegal, and climbers generally find the long arm of the law waiting for them at the top. This, however, does not stop the leading exponents completing often breathtaking climbs. These include Frenchman Alain Robert, who has climbed the Empire State Building in New York, the Golden Gate Bridge in San Francisco, the Sears Tower in Chicago and the Petronas Towers in Kuala Lumpur, Malaysia – the tallest buildings in the world. George Willig climbed one of the World Trade Centre towers and Harry and Simon Westaway scaled Big Ben as an anti-war protest for Greenpeace.

I'M A RAMBLER ...

Ramblers are often regarded with anything from suspicion to downright loathing, but with 130,000 members in the UK there is no doubting the popularity of the pastime.

According to the Ramblers' Association, the aims of enthusiasts are to:

- encourage walking
- protect rights of way (footpaths)
- defend the beauty of the countryside
- campaign for freedom to roam over uncultivated open country

It is this latter aim that has brought the rambling fraternity into such conflict with landowners. In 1932 the Manchester Rambling Association organised a mass trespass of 3,000 walkers to protest at fell land near Kinder Scout in Derbyshire being closed to the public. There ensued a pitched battle with gamekeepers armed with clubs and truncheon-wielding policemen, and many of the ramblers were jailed. The protest worked, however, and a plaque in the Edale Tourist Information office celebrates both the trespass and the classic song 'Manchester Rambler' written by folk singer Ewan McColl, which goes:

I'm a rambler, I'm a rambler from Manchester way,
I get all my pleasure the hard moorland way,
I may be a wage slave on Monday,
But I am a free man on Sunday.

After years of campaigning, ramblers now have a legal right of access on foot to many of England and Wales's most dramatic landscapes. This new legal right – or freedom to roam – provided by The Countryside and Rights of Way Act 2000, applies only to certain areas of uncultivated open country namely mountain, moor, heath, down and registered common land.

A LOT LESS BOVVER WITH A HOVER

The Hovercraft Club of Great Britain was started in 1960 by a group of enthusiasts who wanted to develop single seat hovercraft for racing or recreational cruising on rivers and coastal waters. It now has 700 members nationwide and organises events throughout the year. The races, in which the hovercraft are divided into Formulas – from the powerful F1, capable of up to 80mph, to F25 small craft which can be both raced and used for recreational cruises on rivers and coastal waters – have proved most popular.

FLYBALLERS DO IT DOGGY-STYLE

This is the perfect sport for dog lovers, for despite its name and the fact it is a team sport, Flyball relies almost entirely on canine athletic ability and ball-handling skills. In fact the only 'skill' the human part of the team needs is the ability to select four dogs from a squad of six to compete. Flyball takes the form of a relay race, with teams competing over a course of four hurdles. At the far end of the course the first dog retrieves a ball from a box before racing back to the start when the next dog goes. The winning team is the first to get all four dogs to complete the course without any faults.

ENDURO

If you're the type of person who finds the Le Mans 24-hour race a breeze, then Enduro could be the sport for you. Essentially it is a long-distance off-road endurance event where competitors keep to time schedules between checkpoints. The sport originated in 1913 when the International Six Days was run to test the reliability and endurance of man and machine. Most modern Enduros are of one or two days in duration and last up to eight hours per day covering around a hundred miles – usually a number of laps of the same hilly, woodland course. Competitors lose points for being early or late at checkpoints and ties are decided at special tests of either a motocross circuit or cross country route with competitors timed on these tests to one hundredth of a second.

HORSING AROUND

Frenchman Jean-Paul Depons loved horse riding, rugby and basketball in equal measure. So, in order not to miss out on any, he invented Horseball.

Two opposing teams of six riders and horses are required to gain possession of a ball, specially fitted with six leather handles, and pass it at least three times between themselves as they race towards the goal. Points are scored by firing the ball through a hoop, one metre in diameter, suspended on a 3.5m pole.

The game is played in two halves, each of ten minutes, with half-time of three minutes. It is umpired by two referees, one on horseback and the other on a chair at the side of the pitch.

A huge hit in France, the sport has recently crossed the channel to the UK, where increasing numbers of equestrian clubs are taking it up as a means not only of enjoyment, but of improving their horse-handling technique.

MUZZLE-LOADERS AND MUZZLE-LOADING

Flintlocks, percussion revolvers and duelling pistols may have been superseded by Uzis and Kalashnikovs as the weapon of choice on the battlefield, but that hasn't stopped hundreds of enthusiasts enjoying the crash, bang, wallop of old-style firearms. The Muzzle Loaders Association of Great Britain, formed in 1952, has its own ranges on the outskirts of Warwick, where it's possible to enjoy supervised shooting and take part in competitions.

PÈTANQUE

When two balls and a jack were unearthed in the sarcophagus of an Egyptian Prince of the 52nd century BC, it gave fans of *Pétanque* just claims as the oldest sport in the world.

But of course, they have always known that this form of bowls is renowned throughout history. The game is documented in France and England at the times of Edward III (1312–77), while it's highly likely a form of *Pétanque* was being played by Sir Francis Drake at Plymouth Hoe when he was informed of the arrival of the Spanish Armada. As its name suggests, however, the modern form of the game was developed in 1910 in the small town of La Ciotat, near Marseilles. The concept of the game of *Pétanque* is simple and similar to bowls, i.e. resting your *boule* closer to the jack than your opponent. However, instead of rolling wooden bowls over an immaculately maintained lawn, *Pétanque* is played on an easily maintained area of fairly level 'rough' ground, with a metal *boule* rolled or spun towards the jack.

ROCK-IT-BALL

Launched in 2005, Rock-It-Ball – the New Age equivalent of Dodgeball – is *the* sport which is taking school gymnasiums by storm. The sport is played with a 'Rock-It' – a control bar with a thrower/catcher on each end. It can be played in several ways, but the format that is proving most infectious features two teams of four players firing low-impact balls at each other. Hitting the opponent with a ball scores one point, but if the opponent catches and maintains hold of the ball in his catcher he gets two points. Where the game scores highly with teachers is that kids can't simply loiter at the edge of the playing area as they might in football and rugby. If they do, they are likely to be hit by the ball.

TOUR DE FRANCE TIMES

The first winner of the Tour de France was Maurice Garin in 1903. Garin covered the gruelling 2,428km course in 94hrs 33mins – an average speed of 25.7kph. Such has been the improvement in roads and bike technology since then, that if Garin had ridden the 2005 Tour at the same pace he would have finished more than 54 hours behind winner Lance Armstrong. The following table shows just how the world's toughest race has got faster.

Year	Distance	Time	Ave Speed	Winner
1903	2,428km	94hr 33min	25.679kph	Maurice Garin
1926	5,745km	38hr 44min	24.063kph	Lucien Buysse
1947	4,922km	147hr 10min	33.404kph	Gino Bartali
1999	3,686km	91hr 32min	40.276kph	Lance Armstrong
2005	3,607km	86hr 15min	41.654kph	Lance Armstrong
2006	3,657km	89hr 39min	40.600kph	Floyd Landis

C B FRY: SUPERSPORTSMAN

The great C B Fry was a man who could have turned his hand to any of the sports and pastimes featured in this book and been effortlessly brilliant at them. As it was, at the end of the nineteenth century Fry concentrated his efforts on the major sports of cricket, football, rugby and athletics and became a leading player in all of them. Today, fifty years after his death, his achievements remain astonishing and, in the modern era of professional sport, unlikely to ever be repeated:

- Football: played for Oxford University, Corinthians, and Southampton – for whom he appeared in the 1902 FA Cup final
- Rugby Union: played for Oxford University, Blackheath and the Barbarians
- Athletics: equalled the world long-jump record of 23ft 6.½in (7.18m) in 1892
- Cricket: scored six consecutive centuries for Sussex in a first-class career in which he averaged over 50. He also played for England

THE DANGEROUS SPORTS CLUB[1]

The Dangerous Sports Club was founded by extreme sports enthusiasts David Kirke, Chris Baker and Ed Hulton. The club first burst onto the national consciousness in 1979 when they performed the first recorded bungee jump (as mentioned below). The ensuing publicity encouraged them to even more daring and surreal feats of madness, including descending an Alpine mountain in a double-decker bus, hang-gliding from active volcanoes, microlight flying and perfecting an early form of BASE jumping.

The club still exists, although the upsurge in popularity of the extreme sports they created has meant that their activities no longer get the publicity they once did.

BUNGEE JUMPING

In the 1950s a BBC documentary featured the 'land-divers' of Pentecost Island in Vanuatu. These were young tribesmen who jumped from tall wooden platforms with vines attached to their ankles and, remarkably, survived without ripping their legs off. Inspired by this, in 1979 members of the Dangerous Sports Club created a more user-friendly version of land-diving, in which the unforgiving vines were replaced by elastic cord. That same year four members jumped off the 250ft Clifton Suspension Bridge in Bristol and the sport of bungee jumping was born. Needless to say they were immediately arrested – but this did not stop enthusiasts across the world taking up the challenge. Today bungee jumping is amazingly popular, and has spread from bridges and cranes to hot air balloons and even helicopters.

WHAT A DRAG

Always a favourite of Saturday afternoon's *World of Sport*, drag racing has dipped from the public eye somewhat since its heyday in the 1970s. However, it remains a hugely popular pastime in the USA, where it originated. Essentially the idea is to complete a short, straight and level course in the shortest amount of time, starting from a dead stop. The most common distance is one quarter of a mile (1320ft / 402m), although tracks half this distance are also popular. In order to generate the huge acceleration needed, drag cars tend to have huge back wheels and engine housings tapering away to needle-thin front ends, although modified sports cars are also used in certain categories.

ELEVATOR SURFING

Is it a sport? Is it a pastime? Or is it simply a death wish? The jury is out on elevator surfing, but needless to say this is one activity you shouldn't try at home unless you either know what you are doing or you are mentally unstable. As the name suggests, elevator surfers get their kicks from riding moving elevators from the outside, i.e. on the roof. Typically, office buildings and university campuses tend to be the most popular locations for this highly illegal and dangerous activity. But whatever thrills can be obtained from elevator surfing tend to be overshadowed by the likelihood of gruesome death for those who get it wrong. Several enthusiasts have already been killed after being crushed between the elevator and the top, sides or bottom of the shaft, being struck by the counterweight, or simply sliding off the elevator and plunging several floors to their deaths.

MOUNTAIN UNICYCLING

Mountain unicycling is the inevitable progression from off-road mountain-biking. Although scorned, enthusiasts claim that unicycling is a far more physically challenging sport, and point to the fact that unicycles are direct drive, and therefore the rider is always pedalling whether uphill or downhill. Just to make life even more complicated, tandem versions are often seen.

KITE SURFING, KITE BOARDING, SNOW KITING

When it comes to thrill-seeking, man's ingenuity knows no bounds. Kites have been around for centuries, and for centuries a key aspect of the popular pastime has been for the kite flyer to keep his or her feet firmly planted on the ground. In recent years, however, a hardy bunch of enthusiasts have taken to utilising the pulling power of the kite by attaching themselves to moving objects and being dragged along at high speed. Known as kite surfing, the sport began by combining large kites with traditional surfboards. The sport soon evolved, and now special 'power kites' are used in tandem with small, lightweight and manouverable boards known as 'wakeboards'. This enables the kite surfer to literally skip over the surface of the water, and often leave it in order to perform intricate mid air acrobatics. In a strong wind with flat water, it's possible to traverse at 50kph (30mph) or more.

It doesn't stop there, though. Just as skateboards developed as a land-based version of the surfboard, 'kite boards' are oversized skateboards with large, robust wheels designed to travel over rough terrain and sand. The introduction of 'snow kites' – lightweight sledges designed to be pulled by a kite on the snow – means that what began as a summer sport can now be practised all year round.

IN CELEBRATION OF REAL TENNIS

Let cricketers wait the tardy sun
Break one another's shins and call it fun;
Let Scotia's golfers through the affrighted land
With crooked knee and eyeball stand;
Let football rowdies show their straining thews
And tell their triumphs to a mud-stained Muse;
Let india-rubber pellets dance on grass
Where female arts the ruder sex surpass;
Let other people play at other things;
The king of games is still the game of Kings.
– James Kenneth Stephen

MORNINGTON CRESCENT

The BBC Radio 4 panel show *I'm Sorry I Haven't A Clue* was first broadcast in 1972 and since then has become something of a cult, with its blend of irreverent humour, biting satire and saucy one-liners. The structure of the show – such as it is – is based around a series of light-hearted games, such as 'One Song Sung To The Tune Of Another', 'Killer First Lines', and 'Ancient Radio Times' featuring programmes listed in the Ancient Greek version of the *Radio Times*. By far the most famous *ISIHGAC* game, however, is 'Mornington Crescent'.

Named after the Mornington Crescent tube station in London, it consists of moves between stations on the London Underground, the winner being the first to reach Mornington Crescent. The game's secretive, complex-sounding rules and dramatic manner of play are intended to parody self-important strategy games, and are perhaps best summed up by this explanation from regular panellists Graeme Garden, Tim Brooke-Taylor and Barry Cryer.

Graeme Garden: The traditional opener, like the King's pawn really – Oxford Circus, well in the zone, and gives you limited access to Northern parallels. But I suppose it is technically laying an offside trap there. Force the next player into *Knip* if he is not very careful.

Tim Brooke-Taylor: So I have to go Vauxhall. Basically, things have changed slightly since the Millennium Bridge was put there, so you can back double. So it is basically a *Reverse* move.

Barry Cryer: I'm going Regent's Street, because that is bridging Oxford Circus and Piccadilly Circus. So it is an absolute definitive *Lateral*, which you can reverse on if the situation is right, so you have a double value. It is a *Bridger*, it is a *Lateral*, a very useful one early on.

TEN COMMANDMENTS OF GOLF ETIQUETTE

1. Tee. One player on the tee at a time. It is a breach of etiquette to stand behind a golfer on the tee, or anywhere else on the golf course. Joining them on the tee to watch the shots is also a breach of etiquette. It is also a breach of etiquette to pound your tee into the ground or to leave it embedded in the teeing ground.

2. Speed of play. Always play without delay at all times. Don't lag behind or crowd unnecessarily the group in front. Never talk or tell stories that in anyway, even for a few seconds, delay play. Consider the scorecard after hitting, while proceeding to the next shot, never on the tee or green.

3. Cart use. Golf carts should speed up play not slow it down. After the tee shot, proceed to the first ball and drop off the player, then proceed, safely, to the other ball. The dropped-off player should take extra clubs, if there is any doubt.

4. Gimmies and Mulligans. Never give a shot that matters unless it is beyond the realm of remote possibility that the player could miss it. Mulligans, where a player is allowed to retake a duffed shot, are never allowed.

5. Bunkers. When you leave a bunker you should remove all evidence that you were ever there.

6. On The Green. Fix your ball marks like a craftsman, leaving no bare ground and an even, smooth surface where the ball mark was. Never dig under a ball mark and lever the soil upwardly with your tee or tool – pull the surrounding grass gently to the middle of the mark, starting at the highest point.

7. When another player is addressing the ball. There are only two things that every other player should be doing when a player is addressing the ball: standing absolutely still and watching the player hit. Movement is unacceptable. Talking is unacceptable. Fussing with equipment is unacceptable. Looking around is unacceptable. Stand still and watch the shot. If you can't render this simple courtesy, then you do not belong on a golf course.

8. Clearly state your score when holed out. Making other players ask what you had on the hole is a breach of etiquette.

9. Settling up. Always have the exact amount needed to settle the game. Saying, 'Do you have change for a twenty?' is a breach of etiquette.

TEN COMMANDMENTS OF GOLF ETIQUETTE (CONTINUED . . .)

10. Temperament. You are never out of it until you give up. Play like a gentleman, in demeanour and attitude, because in golf it is not what happens to you, it's your attitude towards it that determines the ultimate outcome.

FLICK TO KICK

Long before the advent of hi-tech video games, the only way to replicate the thrills and spills of soccer in your own living room was to buy a Subbuteo table football set. Invented in 1947 by Peter Adolph, the game was originally going to be called 'The Hobby', until copyright laws forced a rethink. Not to be outdone, Adolph discovered that the hobby was also the name of a bird of prey, whose Latin name was *subbuteo*.

Early versions were basic: sets consisted of two cardboard teams, a celluloid ball and metal goalposts with paper nets. There was no pitch – people were advised to chalk lines on an old Army-issue blanket. At the peak of Subbuteo's popularity in the 1970s there were more than 300 teams to choose from, plus a range of accessories including throw-in figures, TV gantries and stadiums. A survey in 2002 revealed that 90 per cent of fathers over the age of 30 owned Subbuteo sets when they were boys.

In 1978 Irish band The Undertones immortalised Subbuteo by mentioning it in their hit 'My Perfect Cousin', which contained the lines: 'He always beat me at Subbuteo 'cos he flicked to kick and I didn't know.'

A SELECTION OF (CLEAN) FOOTBALL CHANTS

ARSENAL

You are my Arsenal, my only Arsenal,
You make me happy when skies are grey,
You'll never notice how much I love you,
Please don't take my Arsenal away.

CHARLTON ATHLETIC

Valley Floyd Road, the mist rolling in from the Thames,
My desire, is always to be found at Valley Floyd Road.
Many miles have I travelled, many games have I seen,
Following Charlton my favourite team,
Many hours have I spent in the Covered End Choir,
Singing Valley Floyd Road, my only desire.

CHELSEA

Flying high up in the sky,
We'll keep the blue flag flying high,
From Stamford Bridge to Wemb(er)ley,
We'll keep the blue flag flying high.

EVERTON

Oh we hate Bill Shankley and we hate St John, but most of all we
hate big Ron, And we'll hang the Kopites one by one, on the banks
of the royal blue Mersey.
Oh to hell with Liverpool and Rangers too, throw them all in the
Mersey, And we'll fight, fight, fight with all our might for the boys
in the royal blue jerseys.

A SELECTION OF (CLEAN) FOOTBALL CHANTS (CONTD...)

LIVERPOOL

When you walk through a storm,
Hold your head up high,
And don't be afraid of the dark,
At the end of a storm,
There's a golden sky,
And the sweet silver song of a lark,
Walk on through the wind,
Walk on through the rain,
Though your dreams be tossed and blown,
Walk on, walk on, with hope in your heart,
And you'll never walk alone,
You'll never walk alone.

NEWCASTLE UNITED

Oh, my lads you should've seen us gannin',
Gannin' along the Scotswood Road just to see them stannin',
All the lads and lasses there, all with smiling faces,
Gannin' along the Scotswood Road to see the Blaydon Races!

WEST HAM UNITED

I'm forever blowing bubbles, pretty bubbles in the air,
They fly so high, nearly reach the sky,
Then like my dreams they fade and die,
Fortune's always hiding, I've looked everywhere,
I'm forever blowing bubbles, pretty bubbles in the air,
United! United!

WHAT A RACKET

Although not to be confused with racketeering, the game of rackets has less than auspicious origins. It began among inmates of London's King's Bench and Fleet debtors' prisons in the eighteenth century, and was based on the public-school game of fives. The prisoners modified the game by using tennis rackets to speed up the action. They played against the prison wall, sometimes at a corner to add a side wall to the game. Racquets – as it was then known – subsequently became popular outside the prison, played in alleys behind pubs. Ironic, then, that one of the finest exponents of the game should be the thoroughly blue-blooded Lord Aberdare, AKA the Hon. Charles Napier Bruce (1885–1957), who played for Winchester College, Oxford University and Middlesex, and won the British amateur singles title in 1922 and 1931, and the doubles crown ten times between 1921 and 1934.

CRAZY WALKERS

Most of us enjoy a brisk stroll now and again, and some even like to take in the odd hill or two. But in Switzerland the annual Airolo–Chiasso relay takes walking into the realms of masochism. Held in October over a total distance of 115km (72 miles) the event is a five-man relay against the clock, and includes hairpin bends, perilous descents and sheer mountain climbs. Despite this, the event attracts international fields – although strangely enough it is usually won by the Swiss and their immediate neighbours the Italians.

EVOLUTION OF DARTS

Prior to 1949 the game of darts was very much a hit-and-miss affair, largely due to the erratic nature of the darts themselves. Most were made of wood or metal, with feather flights that had a tendency to fall to pieces after a few games. In 1949, however, Unicorn took a major step towards improving performance when it became the first company to sell darts classified by actual weight. Six years later they introduced one-piece plastic flights and, in the early 1970s, to coincide with the upsurge in interest in the game, the firm went one step further by introducing the first commercial tungsten alloy darts, which allowed the player the advantage of slimmer darts for closer grouping.

Today, 21st century dart technology means that top darters are equipped with arrows with rotating, interchangeable integral steel shafts and rotating, retracting and instantly interchangeable dart points. The oche will never be the same again.

TALLEST BASKETBALL PLAYERS

Suleiman Ali Nashnush	(tallest basketball player ever, born Libya), 8ft 5in
Manute Bol	(ex-National Basketball Association [NBA]), 7ft 7in
Gheorghe Muresan	(ex-NBA and star of the movie *My Giant*), 7ft 7in
Shawn Bradley	(NBA), 7ft 6in
Yao Ming	(NBA), 7ft 6in
Malgorzata 'Margo' Dydek	(tallest player in the Women's NBA), 7ft 2in
Kareem Abdul Jabbar	(ex-NBA), 7ft 2ins
Nathan Popp	(University of Northern Carolina), 7ft 2in
Frederic Weiss	(France), 7ft 2in
Wilt Chamberlain	(ex-NBA and tallest volleyball player ever), 7ft 1in

COST OF POLO

Polo is a sport traditionally associated with the idle rich – and for good reason. For the beginner, an experienced horse costs from between £1,500 and £2,500. He will require shoeing every six to eight weeks at a cost of £30 to £50 and vet bills usually total £200 to £300 annually. Stabling and feed bills range from £150 to £300 per month. A basic playing uniform for the horse comprises at least one saddle (£300–£700), bridles (£150 each), blankets and polo wraps (£40). You need a helmet (£60), boots (£90), kneeguards (£40) and mallets (£50). Other expenses will include grounds fees (£300 and up) and membership of your national polo association (about £100). So, if you've got around £8,000 spare, then polo could be the game for you if not, then stick to the mints!

BEAR-BAITING

Bear-baiting – in which packs of dogs are let loose on defenceless bears – may sound abhorrent today, but the sport was all the rage for more than 800 years in Britain. In fact, in the sixteenth century, a crown office, Master of the Bears, earned its occupant a stipend of 16d (just under 7p) per day. There were bear gardens in London, notably one behind Shakespeare's Globe Theatre and in the Royal Palace. Mary Tudor and her sister Elizabeth were great fans. Robert Laneham, writing in 1575, claimed it was '…a sport very pleasant to see the bear, with his pink eyes learing after his enemies approach … if he were taken once, then by what shift, with clawing, with roaring, with tossing and tumbling he would work himself from them … with the blood and slaver hanging about his physiognomy.'

THE STAMFORD BULL RUNNING

With its origins as far back as King John, the Stamford bull running was held every November in the Leicestershire market town. The unfortunate bull would be let loose in the streets, then chased by inhabitants armed with sticks and clubs. The hunt lasted all day and the exhausted animal was eventually surrounded, killed and eaten. Various attempts to stop the event ended in failure, including one intervention by the Society for the Prevention of Cruelty to Animals that led to a riot. It was not until 1840 that the Stamford Bull Run was finally ended.

BADMINTON

Badminton is named after the seat of the Duke of Beaufort at Badminton in Gloucestershire, where the game allegedly evolved in the 1870s from the ancient children's game of battledore and shuttlecock. It was hugely popular with the officer classes, who took it to India and played it outdoors over a few pink gins. Indeed it was in Poona, India, where the first laws of the game were drawn up – although it would take until 1894 before they were unified under the auspices of the Badminton Association. The game, however, remains accessible to all and a perfect outdoor pastime to enjoy on a summer's afternoon.

BARLEY-BREAK

In the days before organised sport, folk had to pretty much make their own amusement. And down on the farm, that invariably meant a game of Barley-Break. Essentially, it was British Bulldog but with the difference that it was played among the barley stacks in the farmyard. A piece of ground was divided into three parts, the middle portion being called 'Hell'. A man and woman stood hand in hand and tried to catch other couples as they advanced from the outer sections. Those who they caught then had to stand in the middle. The object was to be the last couple caught, which explains the game's alternative name: The Last Couple In Hell.

BATINTON

OK – so you're a badminton fan but you also enjoy a game of table tennis. Why not combine the two by playing Batinton? This odd hybrid is based on badminton – played indoors on a badminton-style court with a shuttlecock – but played with an elongated table tennis bat made of rubber and cork. The game was invented in 1918 by Bombing Officer Pat Hanna, entertainment and recreation officer of the New Zealand Division on the Rhine. His brief was to 'Organise entertainment, lay on laughter unlimited and rollicking recreation'. He also had to do it for 30,000 in a restricted area – hence the fact that twelve games of Batinton can be played in the area of just one tennis court.

BICYCLE POLO

With a half-decent pony costing upwards of £2,000, polo is not the sport of the common man. Bicycle polo, on the other hand, most certainly is. All you need is a robust bike, an old croquet mallet and a football pitch. Invented, one suspects as a joke, in Ireland in 1891, within ten years international fixtures were taking place. Today, the game is played around the world.

SOME NATIONAL SPORTS FROM AROUND THE WORLD

Afghanistan – Buzkashi (the art of picking up a goat while travelling on horseback)

Bhutan – Archery

China – Table tennis

Finland – Pesäpallo (Finnish baseball) is the national sport.

Gambia –Wrestling

Iceland – Glima (Icelandic wrestling)

Japan – Sumo wrestling is traditionally viewed as Japan's national sport, but baseball is today more popular

Korea – Tae kwon do is traditional, baseball is highly popular as is football. South Korea is also a major force in archery, speed skating (mainly short track), and women's golf

Latvia – Novuss (a form of table skittles)

Mongolia – Wrestling

Nicaragua – Baseball

Philippines – Sipa (a sort of volleyball played using the feet only) is the traditional national pastime

Romania – Oina (very similar but unrelated to baseball)

Saudi Arabia – Falconry and horse racing are traditional, but football still draws the largest number of spectators

Thailand – Muay Thai (kickboxing)

Uzbekistan – Kurash (upright wrestling)

DARTS CRICKET

Rules: Two players compete, each representing one team. Players throw for nearest the bull to decide who will bat and who will bowl. The batting player throws first. Any score over 20 with three darts counts, including doubles and trebles. However, any throw out of the board or into the bull area counts as a wicket lost. Batsman can be 'caught' out if the bowler catches a dart that bounces out of the board. This is not recommended.

The bowler then has three darts. A dart landing in the 25 ring counts as a wicket, while one landing in the bullseye counts as two. Once the batsman's team (normally of six) is out, the players swap roles. The match can be played as a 'one-dayer' (i.e. one innings each) or a 'test match' (two innings each).

BLIND MAN'S BUFF

Nowadays it is recognised as a harmless children's party game, but back in the Middle Ages Blind Man's Buff was an ultra-violent street game played by usually drunken adults in which the unfortunate 'Blind Man' often received broken limbs and was occasionally even killed as he was 'buffeted' around by the other players. The game has been around since classical times – records show it was a favourite of the Roman Emperor Commodus – and there are variations of it around the world. In Italy it is known as blind fly; in Germany and Austria, blind cow; in Denmark and Sweden, blind buck. It is also played in Finland, Russia, China, Japan and India.

THE MOVING GRANDSTANDS OF BOSBAAN

Originally intended for the 1928 Olympics, the artificial rowing course of Bosbaan, on the outskirts of Amsterdam, was not completed until the early 1930s. One of the main reasons for the delay was the construction of its remarkable 'moving grandstands'. These structures were built to run on a 2,000m (1.2 miles) road built alongside the water, enabling spectators to follow the action without leaving their seats.

CRAZY GOLF

If you thought crazy golf was a daft way to kill half an hour at the seaside, think again. Every year, more than a hundred entrants take part in the World Crazy Golf Championships. In 2005, the tournament was held at the crazy golf course on the beach front at Hastings, Sussex, where players battled it out over six rounds and two days of fierce competition. The title was won for the third year running by undisputed crazy golf king Tim 'Ace Man' Davies, the former British champion.

TOSSING THE CABER

Throwing a log might seem as straightforward as, well, falling off one – but the ancient sport of tossing the caber is governed by strict rules. The caber itself is a tree trunk of unspecified size but, according to the Scottish Games Association, should be 'of a length and weight beyond the powers of the best athlete to turn.'

In the perfect toss, the caber will revolve longitudinally (i.e. end over end), landing with its base pointing away from the competitor. It should point in exactly the same direction he was facing at the moment of throw (known as a 'twelve o'clock toss'), and not be angled left or right.

Caber-tossers who compete regularly in the same area become familiar with the individual characteristics of each caber, which, once it has been tossed, must never be cut. Indeed the most feared caber of all is the 19ft (5.79m) Braemar caber, which weighs more than 120lb (54.5kg) and was first tossed in 1951.

ETON WALL GAME

The Eton Wall Game is one of the oldest ball games still in existence, and without doubt one of the most obscure. It is played on St Andrew's Day at Eton College, where a red brick wall separates the playing fields from the Slough Road, and dates back to 1717 when the wall was built.

It is probably a good thing the game is restricted to Eton pupils, because its rules are utterly impenetrable – as these examples show:

- Once the ball is in Calx (the playing area), Furking (attacking) is allowed and the attackers may touch up a Shy (scoring one point by lifting the ball against the wall with a foot)

- A thrown goal is the equivalent of ten Shies

- If the defenders gain control of the ball in Good Calx (one of the ends of the playing field) they must try to kick it forward

- In Bad Calx (the other end of the playing area) they may Furk it over the back line, after which they are entitled to a kick-out

- If they fail to do either of these things, a new Bully (scrimmage) forms either where the Shy was touched up or where the ball went dead in Calx

- After all that, the chances of scoring a goal are remote. In fact, it is estimated that one is scored once every two years!

- Other Eton games include the Eton Field Game and Eton Fives.

HARROW FOOTBALL

Just to prove that their privileged chums down the road at Eton don't have the monopoly on bizarre games, the pupils of Harrow and Winchester Schools have their own. Both are called football, although any similarity to the so-called beautiful game is purely coincidental. Indeed, their closest relatives are probably Australian Rules and rugby union.

Harrow Football is played with a large ball shaped like a flattened sphere, on a rugby pitch marked only with a halfway line and with a pair of posts that are only 6yd (5.5m) apart at each end.

The object of the game is to propel the ball between these posts, thereby scoring a 'base'.

The Winchester game is played with a round ball, but on a long, narrow pitch surrounded by netting and ringed with a rope. Here the aim is to kick the ball over the opposition line.

Both games have a rulebook and terminology all of their own, and, like the Eton games, seem to have developed ad hoc over the centuries depending on where they are played. Baffling though they may be, they remain at the heart of the British public-school tradition.

GLIDING

Gliders based on the skeletal structure and wing design of birds were first built in the sixteenth century, but it was not until the 1890s that manned flight was finally achieved. The pioneer was German Otto Lilienthal, who fitted wings connected to a tail made of osier wands and then covered with shirt material, onto his shoulders and took off from a hilltop by running down into the wind, hanging from the framework and landing at the bottom.

Lilienthal's main rival was the British glider Percy Pilcher, who, like the German, flew both monoplane and biplane models and who, like Lilienthal, was killed when one of his contraptions failed in midair. The spirit of both men lives on, however, in the annual Bognor Birdman competition, in which contestants attempt to fly – inevitably unsuccessfully – from the end of the pier in Bognor Regis.

GRASS SKIING

Grass skiing evolved as a means of overcoming Alpine skiing's one natural handicap – namely, that it can't be done when there is no snow. In 1967 a group of enterprising winter-sport enthusiasts working for German sports firm Kaiser developed grass skis, consisting of caterpillar tracks running freely in a frame attached to each ski. Originally designed as a novelty, the idea quickly caught on, and summer visitors to resorts such as Gstaad and Zermatt in the late 1960s would have been astonished to find the grassy mountain slopes full of downhill skiers. The craze reached England in 1970, when Windermere in the Lake District played host to the first international downhill grass skiing contest.

Although not as popular as it once was, enthusiasts still flock to the Alpine slopes every summer to don boots and skis, and brave the meadows.

THE IDEAL GREYHOUND

Once regarded as the sole preserve of the benighted working classes, greyhound racing is today enjoying unprecedented popularity with all the family due to clever marketing and improved facilities.

For those hoping to bag a winner, the words of Dame Juliana Berners, writing in 1486, are still an invaluable guide to what to look for:

A greyhound should be heeded lyke a snake,
A neckyd lyke a drake,
Backed lyke a bream,
Footed lyke a catte,
Taylled lyke a ratte.

HARE AND HOUNDS

Not content with merely going for a long cross-country run, in the eighteenth century the cream of England's public schools decided to beef up proceedings by turning the pastime into a sport. Thus Hare and Hounds was born, in which two boys – usually the youngest and smallest – were despatched onto the course with a ten-minute head start, then run down by the rest of the pack. Curiously, although popular, the sport never took off in the formal championship sense in the way that rugby and soccer did. However, to this day there are many athletics clubs called 'Harriers' after the sport.

HOLARI

When in Turkey, do as the Turks do – and play Holari. But only if you've got a day to spare. It's a game that bears a similarity to hockey, but dispenses with rules, time limits, field specifications and restrictions on the number of players. Essentially, it is a free-for-all in which one team attempts to strike a *holari* – a wooden cylinder or wedge – through the other team's goal using rough and ready sticks. Games can often last all day, and the score is largely irrelevant compared to the fun to be had in beaning a neighbour with the *holari*.

TOP INTERNATIONAL HORSE RACES

Ireland: Irish Sweeps Derby, the Irish Oaks

France: Prix de l'Arc de Triomphe, Grand Prix du Paris

Italy: Gran Premio di Milano, Derby Italiano

Germany: Grosser Preis von Baden, Grosser Preis von Nordrhein-Westfalen

USA: Kentucky Derby, Belmont Stakes, Preakness Stakes

Argentina: Gran Premio Carlos Pellegrini, Gran Premio Nacional

Brazil: Grande Premio do Brazil, Grande Premio Cruzeiro do Sul

Australia: Melbourne Cup, Sydney Cup, Caulfield Cup

New Zealand: Great Northern Derby, Auckland Cup

South Africa: July Handicap, Gold Cup

Canada: Queen's Plate, Prince of Wales Stakes, Breeder's Stakes

HORSESHOE PITCHING

An old English pastime that has survived the centuries, horseshoe pitching is still a hugely popular pub game. At its most basic, the game involves throwing a horseshoe at a stake, with the aim of 'ringing' it. But many pubs have their own special clay pitch, to prevent the shoe from skidding, and matches between rival alehouses is a highlight during the summer months.

ICE YACHTING

At around the same time people were warning that it would be fatal to travel at more than 10mph in an open-topped motor vehicle, members of the Poughkeepsie Ice Yacht Club in the USA were gleefully reaching speeds in excess of 110mph using wind power alone. Surely one of the most exhilarating pastimes, ice yachting originated in the frozen north of America and Europe as a necessary means of transport during the winter. But it really took off towards the end of the nineteenth century with the advent of improved yacht design and lighter materials. Poughkeepsie was one of the earliest clubs formed in the USA in 1865, and today there are hundreds worldwide.

JOUSTING

Jousting is a competition between two riders on horseback in which each rider tries to knock the other off his mount. The sport was at the peak of its popularity between fourteenth and sixteenth centuries, and was originally a form of military training. In the sporting version, the riders are each equipped with three weapons: a lance, a one-handed sword, and a rondel. When one rider knocks the other off his mount, he is declared the winner of the round. If both knights are knocked off their mounts at the same time, it is called a tie – although in the past they would then engage in sword combat until only one was left standing. Jousting *au Plaisance* indicates that the combat is for the pleasure of the combatants and audience of the tournament, and uses a blunted lance tip. Jousting *A l'Outrance* was typically performed during wartime on battlefields and was performed 'to the death' using sharpened lance tips. Death and serious injury could and did result from jousting *au plaisance*. During a campaign in the Gatinois and the Beauce in France during the Hundred Years War between the English and French, the war was put on hold for a joust.

WHEELCHAIR WHEELIE

Originally attempting to raise money for wheelchair ramps in his community, Robert M Hensel of Oswego, New York, set the record for the longest long-distance wheelie in a wheelchair on 3 October 2002. Hensel went around his local sports track in his wheelchair on two wheels continuously for more than two hours, covering a distance of 6.178 miles (9.94km).

CHESS PUZZLER

Readers who enjoy solving chess problems are invited to try this record-breaking problem, published in 1889 by Otto Titusz Bláthy:
White: King b4, Queen d2, Pawn a5, c2, e6, f2, f4, g2, g5.
 Black: King c7, Queen a8, Rook e5, Knight g8, h8, Pawn a6, b7, c4, e4, e7, f5, g6, h4.

The task to solve? Mate in 257 moves!

RUBIK'S CUBE CONUNDRUM

The Rubik's Cube was invented in 1974 by Erno Rubik, a sculptor and professor of architecture in Budapest, Hungary. Essentially it is a cube with 9 square faces on each side, for a total area of 54 faces, and occupies the volume of 27 unit cubes. Each face is one of six different colours, and the object is to manoeuvre the cube so that each side is made up of the same colour. Initially Rubik's invention was regarded as little more than an executive toy.

However, in 1980, the Cube was remarketed and its popularity soared to the extent that some three hundred million of them have been sold around the world. It seemed that every week a Rubik's Cube expert – usually a twelve-year-old kid with glasses – would appear on TV displaying their prowess at solving the puzzle in record time.

The current record for restoring the cube in an official championship is 12.11 seconds, by Shotaro Makisumi of Japan in April 2004. The youngest person who solved a standard Rubik's Cube was John Ismael Ugelstad of Norway, who achieved the feat in December 2004 aged just 5 years and 117 days.

THE KING OF KEEPY-UPPY

Football prowess is not necessarily about scoring goals. Almost as traditional a part of the game is the pre-match routine of keepy-uppy, in which players attempt to display their ball control skills by keeping a ball in the air using their feet, legs and head. Usually this lasts only a few seconds – but in 1995 Nikolai Kutsenko from the Ukraine juggled a regulation soccer ball for 24 hours, 30 minutes without the ball ever touching the ground. The fact that this was the last anybody heard of him suggests that when it came to the real thing, Kutsenko couldn't cut the mustard.

Another football maestro was Israel's Raphael Harris who in October 2000 spun a football on his finger for a whopping 4 minutes 21 seconds.

JOGGLING GENIUSES

Joggling – the art of juggling while running – was taken to new heights in October 2003 when a team of 18 Germans from Hamburg covered a distance of 109 miles (176km).

THE WORLD'S GREATEST GUZZLERS

While half the world starves, there is something obscene about staging competitions in which the winner is the person who can stuff as much food down their necks as possible in the shortest time.

Yet there is also something grimly fascinating about it – which perhaps explains why, in the USA, the International Federation of Competitive Eating has been set up to oversee lucrative tournaments for the world's best scoffers.

Without doubt the current champion is Ray Meduna, who in March 2004 wolfed down 22 1oz (28 gram) doughnuts in just 1 minute 39 seconds. However, there is stiff competition on this side of the pond in the shape of Peter Dowdeswell of Earlsbarton, Northants.

Among Dowdeswell's many feats are eating:

- 45 two-hole, 5.5oz (156 gram) doughnuts in 17 minutes, 32 seconds.

- 1lb. (454 grams) of cheddar cheese in 1 minute, 13 seconds

- 3lb. (1.36kg) of mashed potato in 1 minute, 22 seconds

- 12lb. (5.44kg) of ice cream (partly thawed) in 45.5 seconds

Dowdeswell has also proved that he can drink as heartily as he can eat. His guzzling records include:

- A 'yard of ale' (four pints) in 8.90 seconds

- Four pints of beer upside down in 22.1 seconds

- Two pints of milk in 3.2 seconds

- 90 pints of beer in 3 hours

BASKETBALL

The most consecutive baskets achieved by heading the ball is seventeen by Jacek Roszkowski of Poland. This record was set in Dessau at the 2001 Saxonia record festival. The ball did not touch the ground, or any other body part other than the head.

KNUR AND SPELL

Visit any English county and you will find a sport loved by the locals but unheard of anywhere else in the country. In Yorkshire, a huge favourite is Knur and Spell. The Knur is a hard golf-ball-sized ball that is propelled vertically into the air by a Spell, a mechanical device that is tripped when a foot or club presses a lever. The object of the game is to hit the Knur as far as possible with a club – which is more difficult than it may sound. In the 1960s the sport was briefly popularised when Yorkshire Television organised a 'world championship', largely made up of some of the top Knur and Spell players from around the county. Since then it has returned to being a game largely played in pub tournaments.

KORFBALL

Teachers, it seems, are always on the lookout for a game that will involve the whole class rather than just the sporty few. In 1902 Dutch teacher Nico Broekhuysen devised the rules for korfball, which fits the bill by being aimed at mixed sexes and both older and younger pupils. The game, (which is very similar to basketball and was invented just two years later) is played indoors or outdoors on a court divided into two halves. In each half there is a post with a basket (the *korf*) at the top and scoring is acheived by throwing the ball through the other team's basket. Where korfball differs from basketball is that each team consists of eight players: four men and four women. Two of each take up position as attackers and defenders in each half. After two goals the teams change halves and the defenders and attackers swap roles. The game has thrived to the extent that it is now played in forty countries and has its own world championship.

DRAIN SPOTTING

If you see someone in an anorak staring down at a manhole cover, he is most likely to be a drain spotter. Enthusiasts make notes of the unique serial number of each metal cover, then trace it back to the year and origin of manufacture.

CHILLI EATING

Not for the faint-hearted. For this hobby you need an asbestos mouth, as aficionados gather to munch their way through some of the world's hottest chillies. The hottest is the red habanero, which rates 325,000 on the Scoville scale used to measure chilli heat. This beast can cause mouth blisters, and is 65 times hotter than the traditional jalapeno served with nachos. The hottest ever chilli was consumed in 1994, and came in at a gob-numbing 577,000 Scovilles.

NINE MEN'S MORRIS

Nine Men's Morris is a two-player strategy game with a long history in Europe. Each player has nine pieces that move between the twenty-four intersections of three interlocking squares.

The object of the game is to remove all the enemy pieces. Every time a player forms a line of three (a *mill*) on any line drawn on the board, he is entitled to remove one enemy piece, with the proviso that a piece may not be removed from an enemy mill.

The game also goes under many other English names, including Nine Man Morris, Mill, Mills, Merels, Merelles, Merrills, as well as names in other languages such as Mérelles, Merrills, Mühle, Muehle, Mühlespiel, Molenspel, Jeu de Moulin and Tria.

SLAM DUNKING

The whole purpose of basketball is to score baskets, and the game's finest exponents can often attain balletic heights as they 'slam dunk' the ball through the hoop. It's hardly surprising, therefore, that since 1976 the slam dunk has been a sport in its own right, with marks out of 50 being awarded for technical and artistic interpretation over four dunks. One of the finest slam dunk showdowns occurred in 1988, when Dominique Wilkins took on the legendary Michael Jordan in front of a packed house at Chicago Stadium. After scoring two perfect 50s, Wilkins was leading Jordan as the two players entered the fourth and final dunk. It was now that Jordan attempted the impossible: a flying dunk from the foul line. With the cheering crowd on its feet, Jordan started off running, dribbled four times, then elevated from the free-throw line, hanging in the air for what seemed like an eternity, before ramming the ball through the hoop. The judges awarded him a perfect 50 and the title.

Two years earlier the unfortunate Wilkins had been beaten by 5ft 7in Spud Webb, one of the smallest men to play in the NBA.

CRICKET NIGHTMARE

There is only one way to get better at sport, and that is to practise. In cricket, the invention of the automatic bowling machine has proved a tremendous boon for batsmen, who can adjust the speed and angle of the delivery to replicate almost every delivery in a bowler's armoury. They can, however, be highly dangerous to those gallant amateurs who aren't used to facing high-speed deliveries.

Torquay batsman Martyn Goulding was practising against one such machine in preparation for the 1995–96 season when one 75mph delivery kept low and broke his foot. As he hopped around in agony, the machine spat out another delivery – this one a bouncer which reared up and hit him in the chest, breaking two ribs.

AIRSICK BAG COLLECTING

Some people like to spot planes. Others like to collect memorabilia. And some like to combine both. Next time you feel ill on a plane, just pray your sick bag hasn't been pinched by a sick bag collector. There's a roaring global interest in these items – and there is even an Airsickness Bag Virtual Museum on the Internet, featuring pictures of bags half-inched from all the world's airlines.

TREE HUGGING

An increasingly popular hobby, hugging the nearest tree is a highly recommended stress buster according to Rod Nicholson, of the Centre for Harmony in Gloucester. He claims that people who have tried it are more relaxed, sleep better, and make better decisions at work. 'If we used it widely here, we could cut the NHS bill in half,' he says.

KNEEBOARDING

Kneeboarding originated in Southern California in the mid 1960s when surfers killed time waiting for the big waves by kneeling on home-made boards behind tow boats. By 1970 kneeboards were starting to be designed specifically for being towed behind a motorised boat. In 1983, the American Kneeboarding Association (AKA) was founded and started to produce competitive events. As the competitive scene started up, interest in the sport grew. By 1988, the AKA was given official sports division status by USA Water Ski.

MOUNTAIN BIKING

Mountain biking originated in the USA in the 1970s when road cyclists began to experiment with machines designed to go over rough terrain. (A group in Marin County, California is recognised by the Mountain Bike Hall of Fame to have played a central role in the birth of the sport when they began racing down Mount Tamalpais on old 1930s and '40s bicycles retrofitted with better brakes and fat tyres.)

CHEATS CHEATING

Cheating, sadly, is a part of sport that has been in existence as long as there have been rules to break. Fortunately, in their attempts to gain unfair advantage, cheats have proved brilliantly inventive – and often utterly useless.

- In 1991 officials at the Brussels marathon were amazed when Algerian runner Abbes Tehami came in well ahead of the field, despite looking nothing like the Abbes Tehami who had begun the race. Not only was he several inches taller, but also clean shaven – unlike the moustachioed Tehami on the start line. Investigations revealed the Algerian's coach had started the race, then swapped running vests after ten miles with the real Tehami who was hiding behind a tree.

- It became known as the Black Sox scandal after eight Chicago White Sox players were charged with accepting money from gamblers to throw the 1919 baseball World Series, won 5–3 by the Cincinnati Reds. Some of the eight, including 'Shoeless' Joe Jackson, confessed to a jury and were immediately suspended. On their way out, a young boy is said to have called out to Jackson: 'Say it ain't so, Joe.' (The phrase become one of the most famous in American sporting history, though Jackson later claimed the incident never happened.)

- Maradona, at just 5ft 4in, was eight inches shorter than England goalkeeper Peter Shilton. Yet in the 1986 World Cup quarterfinal the Argentine striker not only appeared to outjump Shilton but head the ball into the net. But all was not as it seemed. The slow-motion replay and, more tellingly, a still picture taken by a Mexican photographer showed that Maradona's left hand had deflected the ball home. 'It was partly the hand of Maradona,' the Argentine said the next day, 'and partly the hand of God.'

- Ben Johnson trimmed four-hundredths of a second off the world record to finish first in the 100 metres at the Seoul Olympics in 1988. Within hours, though, his triumph had become one of the great Olympic scandals as Johnson was found to have taken stanozolol, a dangerous anabolic steroid. Stripped of his title and kicked out of the Games, Johnson raced at the next Olympics after serving a two-year suspension, but was banned for life in 1993 after he tested positive again.

- Having just won the yellow jersey at the 1978 Tour de France, Michel Pollentier was obliged to give a urine sample. According to officials, 'Pollentier began pumping his elbow in and out as if playing a set of bagpipes'. Ordered to lift his jersey, the Belgian did so to reveal an elaborate plumbing system running from a rubber, urine-filled bulb under his arm to the test tube. The practice of substituting uncontaminated urine was reckoned to be widespread at the time.

DOMINO TOPPLING

Led by Robin Paul Weijers, an international team of 81 domino enthusiasts constructed the world's biggest 'domino course' with 4,250,000 dominoes, 3,992,397 of which fell in a chain reaction on 12 November 2004, in Leeuwarden, Netherlands.

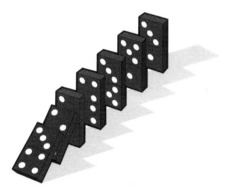

GOOGLY

The googly, one of cricket's most devilish deliveries, was invented by JHT Bosanquet in 1900. He adapted it from the Oxford student game of 'twisti-twosi', in which players try to spin a ball across a table and past their opponent. The delivery made its debut in the match between Leicestershire and Middlesex, where it caused havoc amongst the batsmen. Bosanquet himself was initially unconvinced by the legality of the googly. 'It is not only unfair,' he said, 'it is immoral.'

HANDS WALKING

In April 1968 Walter Cornelius made the 153-mile round trip between Cambridge and London walking on his hands. It took him just seven days.

NEW HAKA

The New Zealand haka, a traditional war cry issued to the opposition before rugby internationals, has been in existence since an All Black team toured New South Wales in 1884. In August 2005, the All Blacks performed an alternative haka for the first time, and in November performed it against England at Twickenham. While appreciated by the crowd, there was consternation that the final dramatic action of the dance appeared to be the slitting of the throat.

Kia whaka-whenua au i ahau!
Hi! Au-e, Hi!
Ko Aotearoa e ngunguru nei!
Au, Au, Au-ë Ha!
Ko kapa o pango e e ngunguru nei!
Au, Au, Au-ë Ha!
I ahaha!
Ka tu te ihiihi
Ka tu te wanawana.
Ki runga ki te rangi
E tu iho nei
E tu iho nei. Hi!

Ponga Rä!
Kapa o Pango,
Au-ë, Hi!
HA!!!

Let me become one with the land!
New Zealand is rumbling here!
The team in black is rumbling here!
Our dreadful power will prevail;
Our ferocity will be overwhelming.
As high as the heavens
is this elemental power,
this force of nature. Yeah!
Silver Fern!
Team in Black!
Yeah!
Silver Fern!
Team in Black !
Yeah!
HAHH!

TRANSFER MADNESS

Today footballers are transferred for exorbitant multi million pound fees, not to mention personal deals and sell-on clauses. Things were a lot simpler in 1937 when Gillingham sold one of their players to Aston Villa for the princely sum of three second-hand turnstiles, two goalkeeper's sweaters, three cans of weedkiller and an old typewriter. It's difficult to tell whether this made him worth more as a player than Daniel Allende, who in 1979 made the move from second division Uruguay side Central Espanol to first division Rentistas for 550 beefsteaks, to be paid in instalments of 25 steaks a week.

BOXING CLEVER

When world heavyweight champion Mike Tyson knocked out challenger Michael Spinks in Atlantic City in 1988 with just eight punches, his income from the fight worked out at $2.5 million per punch.

HOLE IN ONE

The odds of achieving a hole in one at golf are 33,616-1 (compared to the 1-in-14,000,000 chance you have of winning the jackpot on the National Lottery). Despite this, certain clubs in Japan offer their members insurance against just such an event, as it is customary in that country to host a party for the other members and shower them with expensive gifts, as well as planting a commemorative tree on the course. In fact, it is estimated that any Japanese player unlucky enough to score a hole in one will have to fork out in excess of £3,000! Sometimes, a golfer's odds are helped by Mother Nature. At America's Belmont Springs Country Club in 1929, Jim Cash's ball appeared to be stuck on the lip of the hole when a minor earth tremor toppled it into the cup for an ace. Meanwhile in 1934, at the Bay of Quinte Club in Ontario, Jack Ackerman's near miss was converted into a hole in one when a butterfly landed on it.

SERVES YOU RIGHT

In 1912 Jack Johnson, the world's first black heavyweight boxing champion, was refused permission to board an ocean liner sailing from Britain to New York because of the colour of his skin. The *Titanic* duly sailed without him.

SPORTING SUPERSTITIONS

Sportsmen are a superstitious lot. Footballers will often go through the same changing ritual before a game, while golfers have been known to have their clubs blessed before major tournaments. None, though, compare to US baseball player Wade Boggs. 'Chicken man', as Boggs later became known, awoke at the same time every morning, ate chicken before every game, and played 150 ground balls during infield practice. Before each bat Boggs would draw the Hebrew word *Chai* (meaning 'life') in the batter's box, and his route to and from the playing field was so precise that by late summer his footprints were often clearly visible in the grass in the home dugout.

TARGET SHOOTING

The Boer War proved to be a spectacular wake-up call to those who assumed British military supremacy would overcome any opposition. For what the Boers lacked in firepower they more than made up for with superior marksmanship. Indeed, such were the casualties inflicted by Boer marksmen, politicians back in Britain began to seriously question the capability of the army to defend the population against invasion. As a result, in 1900 the call went out for the populace to learn to shoot to defend their country – and in due course civilian small-bore shooting clubs were formed.

Today, despite government bans on the possession of firearms, target shooting remains a popular pastime with thousands of enthusiasts. In fact, shooting with small-bore rifles, pistols, air rifles and air pistols is part of one of the largest participant sports in the UK. There are over one thousand clubs around the country with a variety of indoor and outdoor ranges. Small-bore rifle shooting is mostly carried out over distances of 25 yards (usually on indoor ranges), 50 yards (or metres) and 100 yards, both outdoors. Airgun shooting is at 6 yards and 10 metres.

SCALEXTRIC FOR GROWN-UPS

Most men of a certain age will be familiar with Scalextric, the kids' racing game in which electric-powered model cars are guided round a track with a hand held controller. A select few, however, continue to enjoy 'slot-car' racing long after their childhood years have disappeared. Clubs across the UK regularly stage grand prix events in which enthusiasts can test out their modified machines against the opposition. There are two sizes of car regularly raced, $\frac{1}{32}$th s0cale cars (about 15cm long) and $\frac{1}{24}$th cars (about 19cm long). All models have to resemble a full size racing car, with racing divided between various classes. Most British club tracks have four lanes, but a few have as many as eight lanes. The lap lengths of the tracks are typically between 20 and 50 metres and, like Formula One, every club's track is different.

BASEBALL

Baseball has been played in the UK since 1890, when it was introduced by two men: Francis Ley, a Derby man who got interested on a trip to the US, and AG Spalding, an American sporting goods businessman who saw opportunities to expand his business across the Atlantic. The sport reached its peak popularity in Britain in the years preceding World War II, with baseball teams affiliated with football clubs (hence Derby County's old home ground being named the Baseball Ground). It was run at a professional standard, and games were watched by upwards of 10,000 spectators.

Although the professional era ended with the start of World War II in 1939, the arrival of large numbers of US servicemen ensured baseball continued as a pastime. Today, there are two league teams on US military bases. They are part of an expanding membership of more than forty baseball teams across the country.

THUNDERCAT RACING

'If NASA were to design a Lilo, it would be a Thundercat!' So runs the publicity blurb for one of the more obscure water-based sports. Essentially, a Thundercat is an inflatable rubber boat propelled through the water by a hugely powerful engine. It is crewed by a driver and a co-pilot, whose role is to act as a balance by flinging himself from side to side across the boat as it barrels across the waves. Thundercat racing began in South Africa in the early 1980s when local crews raced inflatable boats down treacherous rivers and along the rugged coastline. It is not a sport for the faint-hearted: with their lightweight structure Thundercats can reach speeds of over 80mph and have a tendency to flip over in choppy seas.

CARDBOARD SHIPS

Talk about making life difficult for yourself! The Great Cardboard Boat Regatta, held annually in Sheboygan, Wisconsin, is exactly that: contestants can only enter if their boat is built from corrugated cardboard. Up to two crewmembers can be used for each boat, which must attempt to navigate a 200-yard course four times. Fortunately, the event is more about taking part than winning. The most prized trophy is the Titanic Award, won by the best-looking boat to end in a watery grave.

CRAZY FROG

Every year more than 40,000 frog enthusiasts descend on Angels Camp, California to take part in the Calaveras County Jumping Frog Jubilee. Top prizes are at stake for the person whose frog jumps the furthest. The cash prize for breaking the world record is $5,000. The current world record was set in 1986 by Rosie the Ribeter, who jumped a massive 21ft 5in.

TOBACCO SPITTING

Not so much a sport as an art form, tobacco spitting is perfected every year at the National Tobacco Spitting Contest held in Raleigh, Mississippi. George Craft was known as the 'Babe Ruth of Spitters' during a long and successful career in which he held no fewer than 14 consecutive spitting records – most in the region of 30ft. When he retired at the age of 75, Craft claimed he had inherited his prowess from his mother who could '… hit the fireplace from any spot in the room and never even got a dab on the floor'.

TIDDLYWINKS

Like many pastimes associated with children (Subbuteo, Scalextric), tiddlywinks has been hijacked by adults and turned into a highly competitive sport. At its most rudimentary level the game remains the same as most of us remember. It is played with sets of small, thin discs (called winks) lying on a surface, usually a felt mat. Players use a larger disc (called a squidger) to pop the winks so that they land inside a pot or cup. However, the formal game has a more complex set of rules, goals and strategies. A core element of this game is the squop, where one wink covers another wink, thereby immobilising it. There are many versions, far too complicated to include here. Suffice to say this upgraded version of the game was introduced in 1955 by Bill Steen and Rick Martin, two non sporting Cambridge students who wanted to play a game at which they could represent the university in a Varsity Match against Oxford. It was a huge hit, and for a while became a cult student pastime. Although competitive games continue to be played today, the zenith of its appeal came in 1961, when Britain's top tiddlywinks team, 'The Twinkies' went on a tour to Africa, where they thrashed a Commonwealth All-Stars team in a match played on the summit of Mount Kilimanjaro!

SOME MORE MAD SPORTS

All-Alaskan Pig Racing (Alaska)
Chicken chariot racing (Seskatchewan, Canada)
Armadillo racing (Fort Worth, Texas)
Pig skydiving (Miami, Florida)

PARAGLIDING

The hills are alive with . . . paragliders. Or so it seems these days anyway, as advances in safety and equipment means what was once a sport reserved for complete nutters has nowentered the mainstream.

A paraglider is a free-flying parachute, launched by running at high speed down a hillside and jumping off the edge of a cliff. The pilot sits in a harness suspended below a fabric wing, whose shape is formed by the pressure of air entering vents in the front.

The sport is closely related to hang-gliding, but relies much more on riding the hot air thermals that rise up from the ground and keep the paraglider airborne. Expert thermal riders can often stay airborne for hours and travel exceptional distances. In 1993 Briton Robbie Whittall reached a height of 14,850ft (4,526m) during a paraglide in South Africa, while in 2006 Canadian William Gadd set a world distance record when he flew an astonishing 263 miles (423km) in ten and a half hours from the town of Zapata in Texas.

THE LIFE (AND DEATH?) OF FAN MAN

On the morning of 22 September, 2002 James Miller left home in Anchorage, Alaska and was never seen again. It was perhaps a fitting end to a thoroughly weird life. Miller, 39, was an avid extreme sports enthusiast who perhaps did more than any other to raise the profile of powergliding – the practice of boosting a paraglider with a large motorised fan worn as a backpack. Such was his notoriety Miller very nearly caused the sport to be banned – his antics even earning him the nickname Fan Man. They also got him beaten up, arrested and threatened with jail.

In 1993 he landed in the ring during a boxing match between Riddick Bowe and Evander Holyfield in Las Vegas. The following year he flew into the middle of the Denver Broncos vs Los Angeles Raiders football game. A few months later, painted green and with his private parts daubed with luminous paint, Miller powerglided onto the roof of Buckingham Palace, causing a major terrorist alert. It was only when he was threatened with a lengthy jail sentence by the Federal Aviation Authority in America that Fan Man finally called it a day.

In 2001 Miller was diagnosed with a severe heart condition and retreated to Anchorage to recuperate. Although his body was never found, it is thought he may have suffered a fatal coronary while out walking in the hills.

BACKGAMMON

In medieval times, backgammon was such a popular game it became a matter of social one-upmanship to have one's own board and pieces handmade by craftsmen. One of the finest boards ever made was discovered in the *mensa* of the altar of the diocesan church of St Valentine in Aschaffenburg, Germany, in 1852. The plain points were pieces of red-veined oriental jasper, which were polished on their upper surfaces. The sides were inlaid, and the contrasting points were overlaid with thick pieces of split rock crystal. The spaces in between the points were covered with thin silver leaf impressed with leaves and other ornaments. The pieces themselves were painted with green, red, yellow, blue and white tints on a gold background, and were designed to represent twin-tailed sirens, dragons and centaurs.

WHY DUMB PEOPLE CATCH MORE TROUT THAN SMART PEOPLE

If you hang around Charley's Hotel Rapids on the Brodheads Creek, or Frank Keener's Antrim Lodge on the Beaverkill, and pay close attention to the inmates, you will notice that the lamer the brain, the heavier the creel.

The reason for this is very simple. When a fisherman gets to the stream he looks it over and decides where he would go if he were a fish. Then he takes out his worm can or his fly box and decides which worm or fly he would prefer if he were a fish.

Then he drifts his worm or casts his fly into the spot he has decided on. If he catches a fish he is very proud, because he knows he thinks like a fish. And naturally, fishermen who think like fish catch more trout than fishermen who think like armadillos or duck billed platypuses or mongooses. Of course, the reason a fish thinks the way he does is that his brain is very tiny in relation to his body. So the tinier the fisherman's brain the easier it is for him to think like a fish, and catch trout right and left.

The same principle explains why fishermen with big mouths catch the most large-mouth bass, and fishermen with banjo eyes catch the most wall-eyed pike, and fishermen with jaundice catch the most yellow perch, and so forth.

The virgin sturgeon has never been caught on rod and reel.

Ed Zern, *To Hell With Fishing* (1945)

COCKFIGHTING

Cockfighting was a hugely popular pastime in the seventeenth, eighteenth and early nineteenth centuries. All large towns had cockpits, and almost all were packed out. Centuries before football, here was the true working man's sport – Samuel Pepys went to one in London in 1663 and found 'the poorest prentices, bakers, brewers, butchers, draymen and whatnot...all fellows with one another swearing, cursing and betting'. In order to cash in on its popularity, unscrupulous promoters often charged extortionate amounts for entry. As a result, those unable to afford to watch the main event would entertain themselves by other means. Throwing at cocks was a favourite sport, especially on Shrove Tuesday. The bird was tethered by a string a few feet long, and passers-by paid to throw stones or sticks at it. The bird would dodge as best it could, but inevitably its legs were broken and it was eventually killed, carried off in triumph by the person who had cast the fatal stone.

The sport was widely condemned, however, with one critic comparing it to 'the behaviour of that silly fellow who boasted of his activity because he had tripped up a beggar who had a pair of wooden legs'.

ONE IN THE EYE FOR THE CUSTARD PIE BRIGADE

Once the hobby of circus clowns, throwing custard pies is now the preferred pastime of political activists. The worldwide Biotic Baking Brigade meet up several times a year in order to splat prominent public figures. So far their victims include World Trade Organisation director-general Renato Ruggiero, Microsoft founder Bill Gates and Tory politician Ann Widdecombe.

A SPOT OF CUDGELLING, ANYONE?

For want of something better to do, in the late-eighteenth century the poor would often break the monotony of their dismal lives with a spot of mass cudgelling. This early team sport featured gangs of the hardest men (and women) in the neighbourhood armed with heavy sticks and wicker shields, fighting against each other until only one was left standing. Sometimes, to make things more interesting, competitors would have one hand tied behind their back.

As befits a sport on which hefty wagers were bet on the outcome, there were rules: 'No head be deemed broke until the blood run an inch' was one of the main provisos.

THE BROUGHTON RULES

Fist fighting, or pugilism, was one of the first sports to have a written code of rules. They were laid down in 1743 by fighter Jack Broughton after one of his opponents had died in the ring, and remained more or less in place until 1867 when the more familiar Queensberry Rules were introduced:

- That a square of a yard be chalked in the middle of the stage; and every fresh set-to after a fall, or being parted from the rails, each second is to bring his man to the side of the square, and place him opposite the other; and till they are fairly set-to at the lines, it shall not be lawful for the one to strike the other.

- That, in order to prevent any disputes as to the time a man lies after a fall, if the second does not bring his man to the side of the square within the space of half a minute, he shall be deemed a beaten man.

- That, in every main battle, no person whatsoever shall be upon the stage, except in the principals and their seconds; the same rule to be observed in bye-battles, except that in the latter, Mr Broughton is allowed to be on the stage to keep decorum, and to assist gentlemen in getting to their places; provided always, he does not interfere in the battle; and whoever presumes to infringe these rules, to be turned immediately out of the house. Everybody is to quit the stage as soon as the champions are stripped, before they set-to.

- That no champion be deemed beaten unless he fails coming up to the line in the limited time; or that his own second declares him beaten. No second is to be allowed to ask his man's adversary any questions or advise him to give out.

- That, in bye-battles, the winning man to have two-thirds of the money given, which shall be publicly divided upon the stage, notwithstanding any private agreement to the contrary.

- That to prevent disputes, in every main battle the principals shall, on the coming on the stage, choose from among the gentlemen present two umpires, who shall absolutely decide all disputes that may arise about the battle; and if the two umpires cannot agree, the said umpires to choose a third, who is to determine it.

- That no person is to hit his adversary when he is down, or seize him by the ham, the breeches, or any part below the waist; a man on his knees to be reckoned down.

ROWING FOR ALL

Before rowing became the preserve of Oxford, Cambridge and the Henley Regatta brigade, the sport was one of the most popular spectator sports in the country, no more so than on Tyneside, where in the mid-1800s the great hero was Harry Clasper. Clasper's exploits drew thousands of spectators to the Tyne, and rowing matches were as avidly followed – and bet on – as modern-day horse racing. An indication of Clasper's popularity is that when he died in 1870, his funeral was held on a Sunday to allow the working man to attend. It is said that over 130,000 lined the streets that day to witness the largest funeral ever seen on Tyneside.

ROYAL TURKEY SHOOT

Although not officially the Sport of Kings, successive generations of British monarch have liked nothing better than bagging a brace or ten of pheasant. Edward VII was particularly partial to game shooting; according to one account, in 1908, he attended a shooting party hosted by Lord Iveagh which consisted of 'seventy men catering for the game, a hundred beaters for perhaps eight guns, two loaders, a cartridge boy and a detective for the King alone. Even the coverts were connected by telephone so the latest information could be obtained on where the sport was best'.

But Edward was nothing compared to his successor George V. During one visit to India George shot 21 tigers, eight rhinos and a bear, then returned to Sandringham where he and six of his friends blasted 10,000 birds in just four days.

HARE COURSING

Until it was banned along with fox-hunting in 2005, hare coursing was a blood sport involving the hunting of hares with specially bred dogs. The primary purpose was to kill the hare. As with all hunting in England, it was initially restricted to nobles, with greyhound and various pure bred dogs being used. The peasantry developed various cross breeds under the generic term 'Lurcher'. The original and underground form saw two dogs released, by a 'slipper' at the same time, to chase a hare, also released in an enclosed area. The first dog to catch the hare won. Although roundly despised by animal welfare groups, around 10,000 spectators used to attend the Waterloo Cup at Altcar, and there were an estimated 3,000 owners of coursing greyhounds.

STREET FIGHTING MEN

By the late nineteenth century, traditional working class sports such as cockfighting, cudgelling and bare-knuckle pugilism had either been suppressed or else diluted by rules. Not to be outdone, the blood thirsty masses turned instead to ordinary street brawls and punch-ups which, under the guise of impromptu prize fights, not only provided entertainment but allowed men (and women) to settle their grudges without fear of reprisal by the authorities.

An example of this was in 1887 when Samuel Fowkes of Leicester killed Arthur Taylor. The two were sworn enemies and had agreed to fight it out after the pub shut. A crowd followed them and made a makeshift ring. Rounds and a 'no-kicking' rule were agreed. The judge thereby determined that Taylor's death arose from a 'fair, stand-up fight' and gave Fowkes just two weeks' imprisonment

THE PERFECT PUB FOR SPECTATOR SPORTS

In 1879 the Astley Arms pub in Seaton Delaval, Northumberland, boasted a bowling track, a quoits alley and a grandstand which could seat 700 people.

HOORAY FOR THE MONARCHY

'There is no place for republicanism in a country where the monarch and indeed her mother are fervent fans of the Turf and love a flutter like the rest of us punters.'
–William Rushton

ANOTHER GREAT LEAP FOR MANKIND

Ever since man walked on the Moon, men on Earth have attempted to replicate the gravity-free thrill of bounding over the ground. The nearest they have come is by strapping on a pair of Powerisers. These are essentially boots with snowboard type bindings, a pivoting foot and a fibreglass leaf spring which enable the wearer to jump up to 1.5m off the ground, run up to 20mph, and take strides up to 10ft.

THE DUELLING CODE

Duelling may seem a simple and quick way to settle an argument, but to reach the stage where the two duellists actually try to kill or maim each other is a tortuous process. The French Duelling Code, drawn up in the 1840s by (among others) the Minister for War, has no less than 84 rules governing how the process is determined. These include:

Rule 7: The offended party has the choice of arms.

Rule 10: There are only three legal arms: the sword, the sabre and the pistol. The sabre may be refused even by the aggressor, especially if he is a retired officer; but it may be always objected to by a civilian.

Rule 16: All duels should take place during the forty-eight hours that have succeeded the offence, unless it is otherwise stipulated by the seconds.

Rule 30: The sword or sabre may be declined by the seconds of a person with only one leg or arm.

Rule 31: The seconds of a young man shall not allow him to fight an adversary above sixty years of age, unless this adversary had struck him; and, in this case, his challenge must be accepted in writing. His refusal to comply with this rule is tantamount to a refusal to give satisfaction, and the young man's honour is thereby satisfied.

Rule 44: When one of the combatants exclaims that he is wounded, or that a wound is perceived by his second, the combat is to be stopped; with the consent of the wounded man, the combat may be renewed.

Rule 47: In pistol duels the nearest distance should be fifteen paces. The sight of the pistol should be fixed and the barrel should not be rifled. Both pistols should be of a similar description too.

Rule 60: The moment one of the combatants has fired, he must halt upon the spot, and stand firmly to receive the fire of his adversary, who is not, however, allowed more than one minute to advance and fire, or to fire from the ground he stands on.

FOR WHOM THE BELL TOLLS

One of the last ever recorded bare-knuckle boxing bouts was between George Camp of Bermondsey and 'Click' Soles of Nottingham in August 1889. After fifty rounds, both men had battered each other to a standstill, but Camp won the £200 prize money because Soles was adjudged to be 'considerably disfigured from his opponent's left-handed deliveries'.

GURNING THE OTHER CHEEK

Dating back to 1266, the World Gurning Championships are held annually at the Egremont Crab Fair in the Lake District. The rules are simple: competitors pull grotesque faces through a horse's collar, the audience applaud, and whoever receives the greatest applause wins. The word *gurn* seems to have been originally Scottish, in the form *girn*, which – appropriately enough – may have been a contorted form of *grin*. It has had several meanings, of which the oldest, from medieval times, is still current in Scots and Irish dialect, and which is defined in the *Oxford English Dictionary* as: 'to show the teeth in rage, pain, disappointment, etc; to snarl as a dog; to complain persistently; to be fretful or peevish'.

PLAIN SPEAKING FROM A PUPIL

'A cowardly, snivelling, ungentlemanlike, treble damnable shit of a headmaster.'
– the headmaster of Westminster School, described by a pupil after he had banned the 1834 rowing match against Eton.

A MORAL DEFENCE OF SPORT

'Through sport, boys acquire virtues which no other books can give them; not merely daring and endurance, but, better still, temper, self-restraint, fairness, honour, unenvious approbation of another's success, and all that ('give and take') of life which stand a man in good stead when he goes forth into the world, and without which, indeed, his success is always maimed and partial.'
– Charles Kingsley

SOME UNUSUALLY INSANE ADVENTURE SPORTS

Zorbing: A New Zealand invention, Zorbing involves harnessing yourself inside an inflatable PVC ball, then rolling more than 650ft downhill. HydroZorbing is an even more bonkers version, in which you run inside the ball when it is floating on water.

Skimboarding: Essentially, this is surfing but without the weight and stabilising fin of a normal surfboard. The skimboard is not only virtually impossible to control – even experts can only remain upright for around 40ft – but highly dangerous.

Landboarding: What could be simpler? Simply fix a set of large wheels to an oversized skateboard, attach yourself to a 40ft power kite and hey presto! – with a following wind and a firm beach you too can travel at speeds in excess of 40mph. Assuming, that is, that you aren't physically lifted from the ground and deposited half a mile out at sea.

River bugging: This crazy sport has been described as the ultimate armchair ride – and it's easy to see why. Essentially, it is whitewater rafting, only instead of a raft you go down the rapids in a one-man inflatable armchair.

FIVE FICTIONAL SPORTING HEROES AND ONE ANTI-HERO

Roy of the Rovers

Finally retired in 2001 after a career that began in 1954, Roy Race was both player and manager at Melchester Rovers and was celebrated for his ability to grab victory from the jaws of defeat in the closing minutes of almost any match. His England debut came in 1963 and subsequently he managed both England and Italian club AC Monza. His was an incident-packed life, encompassing kidnapping, shooting, the death of his wife Penny in a car crash and the amputation of his left foot after a helicopter accident.

Billy the Fish

The star of Fulchester United in *Viz* magazine, half-man half-fish yet with the capacity to deny the boot of any striker in the league. Billy boasted a mullet worthy of Chris Waddle and the strip also featured brief cameos from Mick Hucknall and Shakin' Stevens.

The Oldest Member

The narrator of PG Wodehouse's golfing novels, yet never apparently given a name, this avuncular character rarely if ever seems to lift a club in anger yet dispenses good advice and gently mocking stories such as 'The Clicking of Cuthbert' from his comfy seat in a corner of the clubhouse.

Skid Solo

Formula One hero who figured in the pages of *Tiger* magazine, an aristocratic racer who whizzed through a world of double–dealers and con-artists ably supported by his mechanic Sandy McGrath and apprentice Sparrow Smith. Written out in dramatic style in 1982 after spotting the ghost of his best pal caused him to crash.

Alf Tupper

The Tough of the Track, celebrated for training on a diet of chips and racing in between stints as an apprentice welder, striking more than one blow for the proletariat by outdoing cheating upper-class twits and dodgy foreigners.

Jason Turner

Played by Christian Solimeno in the ITV series *Footballers Wives*, Turner was never actually seen in action on the pitch in spite of his status as the captain of the fictional Earls Park team. He was, however, the husband of the uber-wife Tanya, and there was plenty of action off the pitch what with booze, fast cars, partying and extramarital sex until he plummeted to his death from a hotel roof.

LAST LIME OF DEFENCE

For 158 years Kent County Cricket Club's St Lawrence Road ground in Canterbury boasted the world's only 90ft tall and 50ft wide fielder in the shape of a vast lime tree that dated back to the days when the ground was farmland in the early nineteenth century. Under special rules, any shot that hit the tree was ruled to be a four; a six had to clear the canopy, 120ft in height at one stage before the tree was pollarded in 2000. The last man to clear the tree for a six was the West Indian Carl Cooper in 1992. Sadly, the tree fell in a gale in 2005, but a replacement was planted, to maintain the tradition – although it won't measure up to the old one for many years.

FOUR LONG SHOTS

There have been four winners of the Grand National at odds of 100–1: Tipperary Tim in 1928, Gregalach in 1929, Caughoo in 1947 and most famously Foinavon, who took the 1967 race after managing to stay clear of a vast pile-up at the 23rd fence, which is now named after the horse.

NELSONS

The score of 111 in cricket is referred to as a Nelson, after the celebrated British admiral. One explanation runs that Nelson had one eye, one arm and one leg, but in fact the winner of Trafalgar had both legs intact, and the single bit of his anatomy to which the tradition refers is between his legs. The score is regarded as unlucky unless the batsman lifts one foot off the ground.

TOUR DE FRANCE WINNERS' NICKNAMES

Eddy Merckx	Winner 1969–72, 1974	The Cannibal
Bernard Hinault	Winner 1978–79, 1981–82, 1985	The Badger
Federico Bahamontes	Winner 1959	The Eagle of Toledo
Charly Gaul	Winner 1958	The Angel of the Mountains
Marco Pantani	Winner 1998	The Pirate or Elefantino
Miguel Indurain	Winner 1991-95	Big Mig
Fausto Coppi	Winner 1949, 1952	The Heron
Bernard Thevenet	Winner 1975, 1977	Nanard
Jean Robic	Winner 1947	Leatherhead or The Little Goat
Hugo Koblet	Winner 1950	Le Pedalleur de Charme
Octave Lapize	Winner 1910	Curly
Maurice Garin	Winner 1903	The Rower

CRICKET QUOTES

'Cricket is basically baseball on Valium'
– Robin Williams

'Cricket civilizes people and creates good gentlemen. I want everyone to play cricket in Zimbabwe; I want ours to be a nation of gentlemen.'
– Robert Mugabe

'The English are not very spiritual people, so they invented cricket to give them some idea of eternity.'
– George Bernard Shaw

'It has been said of the unseen army of the dead, on their everlasting march, that when they are passing a rural cricket ground, the Englishmen fall out of the ranks for a moment to lean over a gate and smile.'
– J M Barrie

'When you win the toss – bat. If you are in doubt, think about it, then bat. If you have very big doubts, consult a colleague – then bat.'
– W G Grace

'After years of patient study (and with cricket there can be no other kind), I have decided that there is nothing wrong with the game that the introduction of golf carts wouldn't fix in a hurry.'
– Bill Bryson

'Cricket had plunged me into politics long before I was aware of it. When I did turn into politics I did not have too much to learn.'
– C L R James

'Cricket is battle and service and sport and art.'
– Douglas Jardine

'When's the game itself going to begin?'
– Groucho Marx, watching a match at Lord's

'What is human life but a game of cricket?'
– 3rd Duke of Dorchester (1777)

'Pray God that a professional should never captain England!'
– Lord Hawke

ETON BOATING SONG

The Eton Boating Song is perhaps the most famous of school songs, not only celebrating the rowing prowess of Eton College, but encapsulating the link between sport and education in the nineteenth century. The words of the song were written by William Johnson, a Master at the school. The music was composed by an Old Etonian, Captain Algernon Drummond. It was first performed in 1863.

1.

Jolly boating weather,
And a hay harvest breeze,
Blade on the feather,
Shade off the trees,
Swing swing together,
With your bodies between your knees,
Swing swing together,
With your bodies between your knees.

2.

Skirting past the rushes,
Ruffling o'er the weeds,
Where the lock stream gushes,
Where the cygnet feeds,
Let us see how the wine-glass flushes,
At supper on Boveney meads,
Let us see how the wine glass flushes,
At supper on Boveney meads.

3.

Thanks to the bounteous sitter,
Who sat not at all on his seat,
Down with the beer that's bitter,
Up with the wine that's sweet,
And Oh that some generous 'critter',
Would give us more ducks to eat!

4.

Carving with elbow nudges,
Lobsters we throw behind,
Vinegar nobody grudges,
Lower boys drink it blind,
Sober as so many judges,
We'll give you a bit of our mind.

ETON BOATING SONG (CONTINUED . . .)

5.

'Dreadnought' 'Britannia' 'Thetis',
'St George' 'Prince of Wales' and 'Ten',
And the eight poor souls whose meat is,
Hard steak, and a harder hen,
But the end of our long boat fleet is,
Defiance to Westminster men.

6.

Rugby may be more clever,
Harrow may make more row,
But we'll row for ever,
Steady from stroke to bow,
And nothing in life shall sever,
The chain that is round us now,
And nothing in life shall sever,
The chain that is round us now.

7.

Others will fill our places,
Dressed in the old light blue,
We'll recollect our races,
We'll to the flag be true,
And youth will be still in our faces,
When we cheer for an Eton crew,
And youth will be still in our faces,
When we cheer for an Eton crew.

8.

Twenty years hence this weather,
May tempt us from office stools,
We may be slow on the feather,
And seem to the boys old fools,
But we'll still swing together,
And swear by the best of schools,
But we'll still swing together,
And swear by the best of schools.

THE AMATEUR ETHOS

Corinthian Casuals, founded in 1882 to bring England's best public school footballers together for international matches, firmly believed in the amateur ethos that one should never seek to gain any advantage over an opponent that one would not expect one's opponent to take. This notion of fair play continued even when referees were introduced. The Casuals would routinely withdraw their goalkeeper if a penalty was awarded against them, on the principle that it would be wrong not to accept the consequences of a foul, even if it had been accidental. They are still going strong even today.

One of the foremost advocates of amateurism was the great CB Fry. Fry, who could have stepped straight from the pages of *Boy's Own*, captained Oxford in the 1890s at cricket, soccer and athletics and represented England at each, heading the first-class cricket batting averages six times and holding the world long jump record. He was dead against penalties of any sort, because their very existence assumed that players would 'trip, hack and push their opponents and behave like cads of the most unscrupulous kidney'.

OBSCURE GOLF TERMINOLOGY

Ambrose: a system of team play whereby each player takes a shot, and the ball is next played from the best position. All players then take a shot from this position, and so on.

Baseball grip: grip style with all ten fingers on the club. Also known as the 'Ten-Finger Grip'.

Condor: a four-under-par shot, a hole in one on a par 5. This has occurred on a hole with a heavy dogleg, hard ground, and no trees. Might also be called a 'triple eagle'.

Dogballs: scoring an 'eight' on any single golf hole. The origin of the term is in reference to what the number eight looks like on its side.

Explosion: a bunker shot that sends the ball, and accompanying sand, onto the green. Also known as a 'blast'.

Fat shot: a poor shot in which the club is slowed by catching too much grass or soil, resulting in a short and slow ball flight.

Goldie Bounce: when the ball strikes a tree deep in the rough and bounces out onto the fairway.

Hosel: the crooked area where the clubhead connects to the shaft. Hitting the ball off the hosel is known as a 'shank'.

OBSCURE GOLF TERMINOLOGY (CONTINUED . . .)

Knock-down: a type of shot designed to have a very low trajectory, usually employed to combat strong winds.

Lag: a long putt designed to simply get the ball close to the hole. Or, in the downswing, how far the clubhead 'lags' behind the hands prior to release.

Nassau: a type of bet between golfers that is essentially three separate bets. Money is wagered on the best score in the front 9, back 9, and total 18 holes.

Open stance: when a player sets up with their front foot to the inside of the target line.

Pop-up: a poor tee shot where the top of the clubhead strikes under the ball, causing it to go straight up in the air. In addition to being bad shots, pop-ups frequently leave white scuff-marks on the top of the clubhead.

Q-School: PGA or LPGA Tour Qualifying School – a week-long, six-round tournament in which the Top 30 finishers (of nearly 200 entrants) earn their 'Tour Cards', making them exempt for the following year's tour. Aside from the Majors, Q-School may be the most pressure-filled tournament in golf.

Release: the point in the downswing at which the wrists uncock. A late release (creating 'lag') is one of the keys to a powerful swing.

Sandbagger: a golfer who carries a higher official handicap than his skills indicate, e.g., carries an eight, plays to a two. Sandbaggers usually artificially inflate their handicaps with the intent of winning bets on the course, a practice that most golfers consider cheating.

Through line: When putting, the imaginary path that a ball would travel on should the putted ball go past the hole. Usually observed by PGA players and knowledgeable golfers when retrieving or marking a ball around the hole.

Vardon grip: grip style in which (for right-handed players) the right pinkie finger rests on top of the left index finger. Also known as the 'overlapping grip', most golfers grip with this style. It is named after Harry Vardon, one of the great golfers of the early twentieth century.

Whiff: an attempt to strike the ball which results in the player failing to make contact with the ball.

The yips: A tendency to twitch during the putting stroke. Some top golfers have had their careers greatly affected or even destroyed by the yips; prominent golfers who battled with the yips for much of their careers include Sam Snead and Ben Hogan.

WG GRACE

Nearly a hundred years since his death, William Gilbert Grace remains the name which is most synonymous with the game of cricket in England. He was a batsman of rare skill, who was responsible for developing many of the techniques of modern batting.

In a career spanning nearly forty years, he averaged 39.45 at first-class level, an average undoubtedly dragged down by his playing into his late fifties. At his peak in the 1870s his first-class season averages were regularly between 60 and 70, at a time where uncovered, poorly prepared pitches meant that scores were far lower than the modern game.

A doctor by profession, Grace rarely let his day job get in the way of his passion for cricket. He is said to have dismissed the mother of young twins suffering from measles with the advice: 'Put them to bed, and don't bother me unless they get to 208 for 2.' His debut test match was in September 1880 while his last, remarkably, was some nineteen years later. His record speaks for itself:

	Tests	First Class
Matches	22	870
Runs scored	1,098	54,211
Batting average	32.29	39.45
100s/50s	2/5	124/251
Top score	170	344
Balls bowled	666	124,831
Wickets	9	2,809
Bowling average	26.22	18.14
5 wickets in innings	0	240
10 wickets in match	0	64
Best bowling	2/12	10/49
Catches/stumpings	39/0	876/5

WOMEN CYCLING

'There is a new dawn, a dawn of emancipation, and it is brought about by the cycle. Free to wheel, free to spin out into the glorious countryside, unhampered by chaperon or, even more dispiriting, male admirer, the young girl of today can feel the real independence of herself, and while she is building up her better constitution she is developing her better mind.'
– Louise Jeye, 1895

TIPCAT

Tipcat was a hugely popular impromptu street game played in the mid-1800s. A cross between cricket and rounders, it involved striking the 'cat' – a small piece of wood tapered at both ends – with a stick. The precise rules tended to be made up on the spot, and depended largely on the number of players and the street corner on which the game was played. The game became so popular among the great unwashed that society magazine *Punch* remarked, 'This mania for playing at cat is no less absurd than it is dangerous, for it is a game at which nobody seems to win, and which, apparently, has no other aim than the windows of the houses and the heads of the passers-by.'

DRILL SERGEANTS

In the late nineteenth century, the concept of school games lessons or indeed any form of organised outdoor exercise for children, was unheard of outside the rarefied atmosphere of the great public schools. Instead, inner-city pupils were forced to exercise either in the classroom or in the school hall. There they were lined up and forced to bend and stretch at the command of drill sergeants, who toured schools at sixpence a day and a penny-a-mile marching money.

ORIGINAL NAMES OF FOOTBALL TEAMS

Arsenal – Dial Square
Manchester United – Newton Heath
Everton – St Domingo FC
Tottenham – Hotspur FC
Manchester City – Ardwick FC
Newcastle – Newcastle East End
Southampton – St Mary's
Sunderland – Sunderland & District Teachers
Birmingham – Small Heath Alliance
Fulham – Fulham St Andrews
Bolton – Christ Church FC
Blackburn – Blackburn Grammar School Old Boys
West Ham United – Thames Ironworks FC
West Bromwich Albion – West Bromwich Strollers
Wolverhampton Wanderers – St Luke's
Sheffield Wednesday – The Wednesday
Coventry – Singers FC

Walsall – Walsall Swifts
Gillingham – New Brompton
Wimbledon – Wimbledon Old Centrals
Stockport – Heaton Morris Rovers
Tranmere – Belmont AFC
Cardiff City – Riverside
Bristol City – Black Arabs
Queen's Park Rangers – St Jude's
Oldham – Pine Villa
Plymouth – Argyle Athletic Club
Port Vale – Burslem
Blackpool – St John's
Barnsley – St Peter's
Bournemouth – Boscombe St John's
Rotherham – Thornhill Utd
Watford – West Herts
Cambridge – Abbey United
Leyton Orient – Glyn Cricket & Football Club
Oxford – Headington United

BOWLING A–Z

Alley
Term for lane bed or playing surface. Wood lanes are made of maple and pine boards. Synthetic lanes, first introduced in 1977 as a way of reducing maintainence and keeping longevity, are made from a high-pressure lamination.

Bocce style
Finishing one's approach on the same side as the release, a style used in the Italian game 'bocce'.

Coverstock
Outer shell of the bowling ball. The composition varies from polyester, urethane, reactive resin and particle reactive resin.

Dead wood
Fallen pins that remain on the lane or in the gutter. They must be removed before the next delivery.

Equator
Line around the ball, perpendicular to the vertical axis and the midline covering the entire circumference of the ball.

Finger weight
Imbalance that effectively makes the side of the ball (divided by the midline) containing the finger holes, heavier than the side containing the thumb hole.

Gutter ball
A ball that does not contact any pins because it has been rolled down the lane in the gutter. Zero pins are counted, even if the ball comes back out of the gutter to hit a pin.

Hook
Amount, measured in boards and angle, that a bowling ball deviates from its original trajectory in its path down the lane.

Inside line
The portion of the lane bounded by ten boards on each side.

Kingpin
Either the first or fifth pin, depending upon which country one is in.

Line
Intended path of the ball down the lane.

Mark
A strike or a spare. Also the point on the lane at which the bowler is aiming.

BOWLING A–Z (CONTINUED . . .)

Nothing ball
Defective ball that does not give the desired result, either by fading or deflecting after contact with the pins. Also known as flat ball, dead ball, pumpkin or roll out.

Ovalled hole
The shape of a finger hole being out of round.

Pin action
The manner in which the pins react to the impact of the bowling ball.

Rock
Term for a bowling ball. Also known as 'apple'.

Squeezer
Someone who holds on to the ball with excessive force or muscle. Also known as a gripper.

Turkey
Three strikes in a row.

Urethane
A plastic blend that is normally softer and more porous than polyester. A very popular coverstock before the introduction of reactive resin.

Vertical axis line
A line perpendicular to the midline that passes through the bowler's positive axis point and the negative axis point when extended completely around the ball. Separates top of ball from bottom of ball on the bowler's axis of rotation. Also known as midplane.

Weight block
The dense part of material found in the interior of a bowling ball designed to help create ball reaction.

X
The symbol for a strike.

Zero in
Find the right strike line or spot.

10 POPULAR SPORTS MOVIES

MEAN MACHINE (American Football, 1974)
Burt Reynolds plays a former star pro quarterback turned inmate who organises a game between the cons and the screws.

THE BAD NEWS BEARS (Baseball, 1976)
Walter Matthau stars as a middle-aged loser who becomes a Little League baseball coach. His Bears are a team of misfit kids who eventually come together to win the day.

THIS SPORTING LIFE (Rugby League, 1963)
Gritty, realistic portrayal of a rugby league player that earned Richard Harris an Oscar nomination.

RAGING BULL (Boxing, 1980)
Superlative biopic of boxer Jake LaMotta, directed by Martin Scorsese and starring Robert DeNiro. Boxing – indeed any sport – has never been filmed better.

HOOP DREAMS (Basketball, 1994)
Originally envisaged as a 30-minute documentary, the story of two ghetto kids vying to become basketball stars became one of the seminal sports movies of all time.

ROCKY (Boxing, 1976)
Sly Stallone wrote and starred in this simple but effective rags-to-riches fable about boxer Rocky Balboa.

ESCAPE TO VICTORY (Football, 1981)
A portly-looking Michael Caine leads a team of footballing POWs – including Pele, Osvaldo Ardiles and most of the Ipswich Town squad – in a crunch match against the Germans during World War II. So bad it's brilliant!

CHARIOTS OF FIRE (Athletics, 1981)
The glory of the Olympic ideal seen through the eyes of two British runners. Memorable not only for its feel-good factor, but for the old fashioned amateur ideal that shines through with every step.

WHEN WE WERE KINGS (Boxing, 1996)
A stunning documentary about the 1974 'Rumble In The Jungle' between Muhammad Ali and George Foreman, proving once and for all that Ali is without equal as a sportsman and a character.

SEABISCUIT (Horse Racing, 2003)
A good old fashioned tear-jerker about the little horse and his one-eyed jockey who, in Depression-hit America, raised the spirits of a nation.

KNIFE THROWING

David Adamovich of the USA, also known as The Great Throwdini, broke the speed knife-throwing record on 6 June 2005 in the show 'Maximum Risk' in New York. In one minute, he threw 74 knives around his 'target girl' Ekaterina Sknarina. It's at this point we should mention that you should not try to break this record unless you are an experienced knife thrower.

SNOOKER LOOPY

Snooker was once a sport played in hushed, smoke-filled halls watched by only a couple of dozen spectators. Now it is big business, with live coverage of the main events and star billing given to the top players. That includes nicknames, most of which have been dreamed up over the years by World Championship announcer Alan Hughes.

Nigel Bond: Basildon
Steve Davis: The Nugget
Eddie Charlton: Steady Eddie
Dominic Dale: Spaceman
Ken Doherty: Crafty Ken, Ken-do
Tony Drago: The Tornado
David Gray: The Mighty Atom
Anthony Hamilton: The Robin Hood of Snooker, Sheriff of Pottingham
Dave Harold: The Stoke Potter
Stephen Hendry: The Golden Boy, The Maestro
John Higgins: Wizard of Wishaw
Michael Holt: The Hitman
Alan McManus: Angles
Clark McConachy: Mac
Stephen Maguire: Livewire
Ronnie O'Sullivan: The Rocket, The Essex Exocet
John Parrott: The Entertainer, Mr JP
Barry Pinches: The Canadian
John Rea: King of the Baize
Ray Reardon: Dracula
Alain Robidoux: Scoobie
Matthew Stevens: The Welsh Dragon
David Taylor: The Silver Fox
Cliff Thorburn: The Grinder
James Wattana: The Thai-Phoon
Bill Werbeniuk: Big Bill
Jimmy White: The Whirlwind
Mark Williams: Sprog

BOG SNORKELLING

The World Bog Snorkelling Championship takes place annually on August bank holiday at Llanwrtyd Wells in Powys, Wales and was first held in 1985.

The event consists of competitors completing two consecutive lengths of a 60-yard water-filled trench, cut through a peat bog, in the shortest time possible. Competitors must wear snorkels and flippers, and complete the course without using conventional swimming strokes. Wet suits are not compulsory, but are usually worn.

Llanwrtyd Wells is something of a Mecca for unusual sports. It is here that the annual horse-versus-man race is held, an event which pits runners against horses over a gruelling 25-mile mountain course.

FOOTBALL POOLS HEYDAY

Betting legally on the outcome of football matches first started at the turn of the twentieth century with the advent of the football pools. The idea was simple: for a small sum punters could buy a coupon with all of that weekend's league fixtures. All they had to do was pick out the draws – and eight draws won the jackpot. Although initially run in newspapers, specialised companies soon moved into a burgeoning market. In 1907, for example, a survey carried out in Liverpool showed that nearly 80,000 coupons were collected in a single week. During the Depression years, the pastime reached almost obsessional proportions among working class people desperate to win their fortune. The *Investor's Chronicle* estimated that between 1934 and 1938 pools expenditure rose from £10 million to a staggering £40 million.

THE THRILL OF THE BET

'I have the picture in my mind of a winter's day, when the huge, cumbrous ferry boat, which plies across the Tees, taking the men backwards and forwards from their work, was going slowly back in the late afternoon with the toilers who had finished their day's work. As it reached the shore some other men going across to the works from the town were waiting to board it, among them a man of about sixty carrying his bag of tools in one hand and the evening paper in the other. He stood facing the crowd as, with one question on their eager faces, they jostled across the gangway. And in one word he gave them their answer, the word they were waiting for – the name of a horse. It ran through the crowd like the flash of a torch, lighting up all the faces with a nervous excitement; and it seemed to the onlooker that there was not a man there whom that name did not vitally concern.'

– Lady Florence Bell, *At The Works* (1969)

FLASHPOINT

In 1887 the Lillie Bridge stadium in Fulham, which was used for professional sporting events, was burned to the ground by angry punters. They had gone on the rampage after a race between two of the top sprinters of the day was abandoned because they and their managers could not agree which of them should win!

POWDERHALL SPRINTS

Since it was built in 1869, the Powderhall Stadium in Edinburgh has hosted professional running competitions. In its heyday, at the turn of the twentieth century, crowds of up to 10,000 would pack the terraces to watch the top sprinters of the day in action – and have a flutter on the outcome. The famous New Year Sprint, over 130 yards, featured the cream of the world's paid runners and consequently had thousands of pounds riding on the result. In 1909 a record crowd of 17,000 turned up to watch. Cumbie Bowers of Glenrothes was crowned 2006's winner.

GREYHOUND TRAINING

'As dog-fighting declined in the second half of the nineteenth century, informal dog-racing developed as a more humane animal sport. Dog-racing was a world of its own with all sorts of ways of "stopping" a dog or speeding it up, a rich tradition of potions and tricks passed on from father to son or picked up around the tracks. Handlers would squeeze the poor creature's testicles, jerk its tail, or even feed it a meat pie to slow it down and improve the odds for the next race. When the aim was to win the owners would stand behind the winning line beckoning their "bairns" with their favourite object – a feeding bowl, a bit of blanket, a tin can, a bonnet, a rag or rabbit skin. "Slipping" whippets, as it was called, was quite an art. So was the training of them. A man would set up an old bicycle frame on a piece of waste ground with a cloth rabbit attached to the rear hub by a long string. The father would slip the dog while the son furiously turned the pedals and the creature would race after the 'hare'. Sometimes the tunnel-visioned dogs would crash into the bike itself and require impromptu surgery.'
Richard Holt, *Sport and the British, A Modern History* (1989)

HOW TO RING A RACING PIGEON

A racing pigeon usually wears two rings on its leg. One is a rubber race ring and is put onto the bird for racing purposes. The second ring contains the bird's unique identification number and is usually made of metal and covered with plastic, different colours being used for different years. The ring is placed on the bird shortly after birth and cannot be removed without damage to the ring. Part of the number denotes the organisation of the owner and a typical ring would be GB99J43777. The 'GB' denotes that the bird belongs to a member of the Royal Pigeon Racing Association and the '99' denotes the year of birth. The J43777 is the unique identification number for that year.

LUNAR GOLF

In 1971 Apollo XIV landed on the moon. Inside was astronaut Alan Shepard, who, apart from carrying out the usual raft of lunar experiments, also planned to become the first golfer on the moon – and had brought three golf balls for just that purpose.

Strapping the head of a six iron to the bottom of a sampling instrument, Shepard teed off. In the lunar void, a golf ball hit at a speed of 200kmph at a 45-degrees angle would travel 1.9 km. But the truth is Shepard duffed his first shot, burying it into the dust. His second swing knocked the ball a few feet before it came to a dead stop. Mission Control, providing commentary, said that the shot was a slice. His last shot was more successful, and the ball disappeared in a graceful arc in the direction of a crater. 'Miles and miles and miles!' cried the triumphant Shepard, although its true distance was estimated at 1.4km.

SNOOKER

While the game of billiards dates back to the fifteenth century, snooker is a more recent invention. In the late nineteenth century, billiards games were popular among British army officers stationed in India and players used to experiment with variations on the game. The most commonly accepted story is that, at the officers' mess in Jubbulpore in 1875, Colonel Sir Neville Chamberlain (no relation to the later prime minister) suggested adding coloured balls to a billiards game. The word 'snooker' was army slang for a first-year cadet. This came to be used for novices to the game, and eventually for the game itself. British billiards champion John Roberts travelled to India in 1885, where he met Chamberlain. Chamberlain explained the new game to him, and Roberts subsequently introduced it to England.

LEGAL DARTS

Is darts a sport, or a game of chance? In 1908, the matter was decided officially at Leeds Magistrates' Court. A junior clerk, who had never played the game, was instructed by the bench to have a go and missed the board entirely with two of his first three throws. Up stepped local publican 'Foot' Anakin, who promptly threw three double-twenties twice in succession. The magistrate immediately pronounced the game to be 'skilful' and therefore a legal pub activity.

CAMOGIE

Camogie is a Gaelic sport similar to hurling, but played by women. Two teams of twelve aim to get the *sliotar* (ball) between the rugby-style goalposts by either carrying or dribbling it on the *hurl* (stick).

GAELIC FOOTBALL

Gaelic Football can be described as a mixture of soccer and rugby, although it predates both of those games. It is a field game that has developed as a distinct game similar to the progression of Australian Rules. Indeed it is thought that Australian Rules evolved from Gaelic Football through the many thousands who were either deported or immigrated to Australia from the middle of the nineteenth century. Gaelic Football is played on a pitch approximately 137m long and 82m wide. The goalposts are the same shape as a rugby pitch, with the crossbar lower than a rugby one and slightly higher than a soccer one.

The ball used in Gaelic Football is round and slightly smaller than a soccer ball. It can be carried in the hand for a distance of four steps and can be kicked or 'hand-passed', a striking motion with the hand or fist. After every four steps the ball must be either bounced or 'solo-ed', an action of dropping the ball onto the foot and kicking it back into the hand.

To score, you put the ball over the crossbar by foot or hand/fist for one point or under the crossbar and into the net by foot or hand/fist in certain circumstances for a goal, the latter being the equivalent of three points.

Each team consists of fifteen players, lining up as follows: one goalkeeper, three full-backs, three half-backs, two midfielders, three half-forwards and three full-forwards.

WHY ENGLISHMEN WIN

'Englishmen are not superior to Frenchmen or Germans in brains or industry, or the science or apparatus of war. Their superiority resides in the health and temper which games impart. The pluck, the energy, the perseverance, the good temper, the self-control, the discipline, the co-operation, the *esprit de corps*, which merit success in cricket or football which win the day in peace and war. In the history of the British Empire it is written that England has owed her sovereignty to her sports.'
– JEC Welldon, headmaster of Harrow School, 1881–95

There's a breathless hush in the Close to-night –
Ten to make and the match to win –
A bumping pitch and a blinding light,
An hour to play and the last man in.
And it's not for the sake of a ribboned coat,
Or the selfish hope of a season's fame,
But his Captain's hand on his shoulder smote –
'Play up! play up! and play the game!'
The sand of the desert is sodden red,–
Red with the wreck of a square that broke;–
The Gatling's jammed and the Colonel dead,
And the regiment blind with dust and smoke.
The river of death has brimmed his banks,
And England's far, and Honour a name,
But the voice of a schoolboy rallies the ranks:
'Play up! play up! and play the game!'
– from 'Vitai Lampada', Sir Henry Newbolt (1862-1938)

'Most of the qualities, if not all, that conduce to the supremacy of our country in so many quarters of the globe are fostered, if not solely developed, by means of games.'
– letter from Miss Dove of Wycombe Abbey (1896)

'[He was the kind of man] who made our race pioneers of the world, which in naval warfare won for us the command of the sea, which by exploration and colonization has given the waste lands of the earth to the Anglo-Saxon enterprise...Whilst Englishmen possess this quality they will manifest it in their sports.'
– obituary of mountaineer A F Mummery, killed while climbing Nanga Parbat in the Himalayas in 1895

YABBA FROM THE GABBA

Stephen 'Yabba' Gascoigne was well known as a heckler at Sydney Cricket Ground, where he would sit on The Hill – the grassy general admissions area – and yell out abuse at visiting teams.

Yabba's finest hour came during the notorious Bodyline series of 1932, when England's Douglas Jardine almost caused an international incident by asking his fast bowlers to aim for the body and head of the Aussie batsmen.

Amid the tension, Yabba's knowledgeable witticisms lightened the mood. His best-remembered insults include: 'I wish you were a statue and I were a pigeon', 'Send 'im down a piano, see if 'e can play that!' and perhaps his most famous, telling a fly-swatting Jardine to 'Leave our flies alone. They're the only friends you've got here.'

'The Hill' area was replaced with seating in the early 1990s and the new stand was then formally named *Yabba's Hill* in Gascoigne's honour.

FESTIVE FOOTBALL

On Christmas Day 1915, soldiers from both sides of the trenches met up in no-man's-land for a game of football. Nothing official was kept of this brief meeting between enemies so our knowledge of what took place has always been somewhat patchy.

Bertie Felstead, the last known survivor of that football match, died in July 2001 aged 106 years, but recalled how he and his colleagues got out of their trenches and went across to meet the Germans.

'A football was produced from somewhere. It was not a game as such – more of a kick-around and a free-for-all. There could have been 50 on each side for all I know. I played because I really liked football. I don't know how long it lasted, probably half-an-hour, and no-one was keeping score.'

The truce ended when a British major ordered the British soldiers back to their trench, with a reminder that they were 'there to kill the Hun not to make friends with him'.

PAST WINNERS OF THE BBC SPORTS TEAM OF THE YEAR AWARD

Year	Team of the Year
2005	Liverpool FC
2004	British men's Coxless Fours Rowing Team
2003	England Rugby Union World Cup winners
2002	European Ryder Cup team
2001	Liverpool FC
2000	Jointly awarded – British Olympic and Paralympic Athletics teams
1999	Manchester United
1998	Arsenal
1997	British Lions
1996	British men's 4 x 400m relay team
1995	European Ryder Cup team
1994	Wigan Rugby League team
1993	English Rugby Union team
1992	Steve Redgrave and Matthew Pinsent
1991	Jointly awarded – England Rugby Union team and Men's Olympic 4 x 400m relay squad
1990	Scottish Rugby Union team
1989	British Olympic men's Athletics squad
1988	British Hockey team
1987	European Ryder Cup team
1986	Liverpool FC
1985	European Ryder Cup team
1984	British Showjumping team
1983	Jayne Torvill and Christopher Dean
1982	Jayne Torvill and Christopher Dean
1981	Bob Champion and Aldaniti
1980	English Rugby Union team
1979	British Showjumping team
1978	Davis Cup and Wightman Cup tennis teams
1977	Liverpool FC
1976	British Olympic Modern Pentathlon team
1975	British men's Swimming team
1974	British Lions
1973	Sunderland AFC
1972	Olympic Three-Day Eventing team
1971	British Lions
1970	Nijinsky II team – Horse and Jockey riding team
1969	Jointly awarded – European Ryder Cup team & British women's 4 x 400m relay team
1968	Manchester United
1967	Celtic FC
1966	English World Cup Football team
1965	West Ham United
1964	English Youth Football team
1963	West Indies Cricket team
1962	BRM Motor Racing
1961	Tottenham Hotspur
1960	Cooper Racing

A–Z OF FOOTBALL TEAM NICKNAMES

Can you match the football teams to their club nickname?

NICKNAME	TEAM
Les Aigles de Carthage (Eagles of Carthage)	Tunisia national team
Albicelestes (The White-and-Sky-Blues)	Argentina national team
All Whites	New Zealand national team
Asini Volanti (Flying Donkeys)	Chievo Verona
Gli Azzurri (Blues)	Italy national team
Bafana Bafana (The Boys)	South Africa national team
The Baggies	West Bromwich Albion
Bajen	Hammarby IF
Bhoys, Hoops	Celtic
I Bianconeri (The White-and-Blacks), La Vecchia Signora (The Old Lady)	Juventus
The Black Cats	Sunderland
Blåvitt (Blue-White), Änglarna (The Angels)	IFK Göteborg
Les Bleus	France national team
Canaries	Norwich City
Canaris	Nantes
Colchoneros (Mattress Makers)	Atlético Madrid
Chivas or Chivas Rayadas	Club Deportivo Guadalajara A.C.
Les Diables Rouges, Rode Duivels (Red Devils in French and Dutch)	Belgium national team
Los Diablos Rojos	Club Deportivo Toluca
The Dons	Aberdeen, AFC Wimbledon, MK Dons
Los Ches	Valencia
Les Éléphants	Côte d'Ivoire national team
Geißböcke (Billy Goats)	FC Köln
'Gers	Rangers
Gnaget	AIK
The Gunners	Arsenal
The Hoops	F.C. Dallas (USA)
Jambos, Jam Tarts	Hearts
Järnkaminerna	

A–Z OF FOOTBALL TEAM NICKNAMES (CONTINUED . . .)

(The Iron Stoves)	Djurgårdens IF
Les Lions de l'Atlas (Lions of Atlas)	Morocco national team
Les Lions de la Téranga	Senegal national team
Lions Indomptables (Indomitable Lions)	Cameroon national team
Magpies	Newcastle United
Makrillarna (The Mackerels)	GAIS, Sweden
Matildas	Australia women's national team
Los Merengues (The Whites), Los Galácticos (The Galactics)	Real Madrid
Oranje (Orange), Clockwork Orange	Netherlands national team
O Peixe (The Fish), O Alvinegro (The White-and-Black)	Santos
Panzer	Germany national team
Rams	Derby County
Red Devils	Manchester United
The Reds	Liverpool
The Reggae Boyz	Jamaica national team
Sky Blues	Coventry City
Socceroos	Australia national team
Super Eagles	Nigeria national team
Taeguk Warriors	South Korea national team
Los Ticos	Costa Rica national team
The Toffees	Everton
Los Tricolores, El Tri	Mexico national team
I Viola (The Purples)	Fiorentina

WALES SUPREME

'The great quality of defence and attack in the Welsh race is to be traced to their training of the early period when powerful enemies drove them to their mountain fortresses. There was developed, then, those traits of character that find fruition today. "Gallant little Wales" has produced sons of strong determination, invincible stamina, resolute, mentally keen, physically sound.'

– English newspaper report after the Welsh rugby team won the Grand Slam in 1908.

COUCH POTATOES

In a recent survey, only 14 per cent of the British public who declared themselves to be 'very interested in soccer' actually played the game or were members of clubs. A massive 98 per cent watched it on television, though!

THE AWARDING OF BELTS TO BOXING CHAMPIONS:

The practice of giving out championship belts was started in the late 1880s in the United States by Richard K Fox, publisher of *Police Gazette* magazine. Fox, according to legend, had been insulted by the legendary bare-knuckle fighter John L Sullivan in Harry Hill's saloon in New York City and, as a result, backed a number of fighters trying to beat Sullivan, including Paddy Ryan and Jake Kilrain.

Because the *Police Gazette* was the 'official' source of boxing by Fox's own declaration, he began awarding the Police Gazette Diamond Belt to those he considered champions in several weight classes. One of these, naturally, was Jake Kilrain. In 1889, Sullivan beat Kilrain and was grudgingly recognised as the champion.

Richard Fox died in 1922, the same year that Nat Fleischer founded *The Ring* magazine. Eventually *The Ring* was recognised as heir apparent to the *Police Gazette* as the pre-eminent authority on boxing and would take up the practice of awarding belts.

THE ORIGIN OF BOXING TERMS

Bringing home the bacon: from the four-word telegram Joe Gans sent to his mother when he won the World Lightweight Title in 1906.

Pound for pound the best fighter in the world: first used by a sportswriter to describe the great lightweight champion Benny Leonard.

The Real McCoy: coined to describe middleweight champ Kid McCoy and has several explanations. It's said a much bigger man tried to hit on McCoy's girlfriend in a bar and when McCoy told him who he was the man didn't believe him and laughed in his face. The Kid promptly knocked him cold. When he woke, the would-be bully said, 'That was the real McCoy!' Another version has it that when McCoy fought Joe Choynski in 1899 in San Francisco, to avoid confusing him with another fighter named Peter McCoy who had fought a bout there a few days earlier, the newspaper headline read, 'Choynski is Beaten by the Real McCoy'.

We wuz robbed!: first shouted by Joe Jacobs, manager of Max Schmeling, when at the end of a fight Max seemed to have easily won the decision instead went to Jack Sharkey.

He can run, but he can't hide: the response Joe Louis gave when asked how he'd deal with the speed of Billy Conn in their rematch.

Southpaw: the term for a left-handed fighter isn't of boxing origin, it's from baseball. Early ball fields were built so that home plate faced to the east. That way, the late afternoon sun wouldn't be in the batter's eyes, a dangerous situation when a baseball is thrown in your direction. The pitcher faced west, and if he was left-handed, the ball would be thrown with his south side hand, his 'south paw'.

BREARLEY SNUBS PACKER

'Money apart, Packer is not my style. England is my home. I prefer the chugging British coaster with a cargo of pig-iron to a monstrous supertanker hurriedly constructed. We put up with the buckets to catch the drips in the dressing room at Taunton in order to enjoy the wisteria round the door of the George at Bewley.'
– England cricket captain Mike Brearley explaining why he did not sign up for Kerry Packer's world cricket bandwagon in the 1970s.

CRICKET BATTY

Modern cricket bats cannot be more than 4in wide, according to rules adopted at the end of the eighteenth century. The decision was made following a number of incidents in which batsmen had sought to gain unfair advantage by using oversized bats.

In September 1771, Thomas White of the Chertsey Club turned up for a game against the famous Hambledon team with a bat that was in excess of 10in wide. That same year Mr Garlic, the captain of a local team in Surrey, turned up with a foot-wide bat decorated with paintings of vegetables and garden implements. In order to give the batsmen a sporting chance, he had drilled a hole in the middle, however.

BOXING CLEVER

The Olympic boxing tournament, by dint of the number of contestants and the length of time to complete a bout, is one of the longest in the entire programme. In 1988, it was decided that to save time, two boxing rings would be brought into the hall instead of just one. Of course, it didn't occur to anyone that the bell from one ring would be heard in the other. As a result, some bouts lasted six minutes, KO punches were landed after the bell, and boxers retired to their corners in the middle of a round. Unsurprisingly, the experiment was judged an abject failure by the Olympic Committee and never repeated.

NEVER THE TWAIN

American writer Mark Twain was also a hugely keen angler – although he had little time for the official fishing seasons.

Having spent three weeks fishing in New England, he caught a train back to New York. To pass the time, he struck up a conversation with an elderly gentleman sitting in the same compartment. It did not take long before Twain was bragging that he had over 100lb of bass on ice in the baggage car.

'So who are you, sir?' he asked the old man.

'I'm a Maine game warden,' the man replied. 'Who are you?'

'Warden,' Twain replied, 'I'm the biggest liar in the United States.'

A GOOD WAR SPOILED

Not even the Battle of Britain was going to interrupt members of Richmond Golf Club in Surrey. In 1940, as desperate dogfights took place overhead, the club secretary introduced some temporary rules including:

- A player whose stroke is interrupted by the simultaneous explosion of a bomb or shell, or by machine-gun fire, may play another ball from the same place, penalty one stroke.
- Shrapnel and/or bomb splinters on the fairway, or in bunkers within a club's length of the ball, may be moved without penalty.
- To ensure the safety of its players, the club marked the positions of known delayed-action or unexploded bombs by red flags.

SKYSURFING

It can be argued that mankind's ceaseless quest for increasingly death-defying, not to mention lunatic, ways of passing the time reached its peak with the invention of Skysurfing. If skydiving wasn't crazy enough, in the 1990s some bright spark had the idea of leaping out of a plane at 15,000ft with a surfboard strapped to his feet. The idea behind this madness is that the air can be 'surfed' much in the same way as water.

The simplest Skysurfing technique is to stand upright on the board during freefall, and tilt the nose of the board down to generate forward movement. However, even this basic technique is a balancing act which experienced skydivers find tricky to learn. Performed by experts, there is an undeniable beauty in the freefall aerobatics possible in mid-air, which include loops, rolls and helicopter spins.

SLAMBALL

Slamball is another variation of basketball that has been popular in the USA since 2002. Two teams of four players each compete against each other. Each team has one handler (the equivalent of a basketball point guard), two gunners (guards) and a stopper (centre / goaltender). Shots can be taken from any area of the court, which is surrounded by clear plastic walls. Slam dunks are worth three points, and shots taken from other areas are worth only two. However, the crucial difference between Slamball and basketball is that there are trampolines positioned around the side of the court. These are designed to help offensive players jump to go for a dunk. Contrived? Maybe – but at its best Slamball is one of the most athletic and energetic sports around.

STREET LUGE

Somewhat disparagingly described as 'The Cresta Run for Plebs', street luge takes all the thrills and spills of traditional Alpine lugeing and transfers it to the mean city streets. The principle is the same: competitors launch themselves from the top of a hill while attached to a narrow sled. The fastest time to the bottom wins. However, street luge boards come with wheels, and instead of ice-packed channels the competitors have to negotiate busy suburban roads.

SPORT IN THE WAR

In a bid to maintain morale during the dark days of the Second World War, a succession of representative football matches were organised – home internationals, inter-service games, as well as professional friendly fixtures. They were hugely popular. In 1943 more than 85,000 fans packed into Stamford Bridge to watch a game between Chelsea and Charlton, while on Boxing Day that year a total of 440,000 watched various fixtures. Star man during the war years was Newcastle United striker Albert Stubbins, who scored an astonishing 230 goals between 1939 and 1945.

NINE-DART FINISH

A nine-dart finish is the ultimate check-out in the game of darts, constituting a perfect game. It is notoriously difficult to achieve, even by the game's top professionals.

With each player starting from a score of 501, nine darts is the fewest number of throws necessary to finish the game.

The outshot is traditionally done in one of three ways:

- treble 20 (60), treble 19 (57) and double 12 (24)

- treble 18 (54), treble 17 (51) and double 18 (36)

- treble 20 (60), treble 15 (45) and double 18 (36)

The first televised nine-dart finish was achieved at the World Matchplay Championship in 1984 by John Lowe, who used the second method above as his outshot after scoring two maximum 180s. Phil 'The Power' Taylor is the only player to have achieved this feat more than once on television, having done so three times: the first in 2002, during a quarter final tie at the Professional Darts Corporation World Matchplay Championship in Blackpool, and also in consecutive appearances at the Professional Darts Corporation UK Open Championships in Bolton, in 2004 and 2005.

THE WORLD'S FITTEST MAN

The boom in fitness clubs has meant many former couch potatoes can now use hi-tech cardiovascular machines in an effort to shed those extra pounds. But the amazing feats of Paddy Doyle are enough to give even the most dedicated gym-goer a heart attack. In 2005, at a health club in Solihull, West Midlands, Paddy completed a 12-mile run, a 12-mile speed walk, a 20-mile row, a 110-mile cycle ride, 3,250 sit-up crunches, 1,250 star jumps, 1,250 press-ups, 1,250 leg raises, a 20-mile walk on a stepper machine, a 2-mile swim and lifted a total of 300,000lb at various weights in just under 19 hours – thereby becoming officially crowned the World's Fittest Man.

THROWING FEAT

The furthest throw of an item with an unaided arm was a whopping 1,333ft (406m). That works out at nearly a quarter of a mile. Erin Hemming, 26, from Mendocino, California accomplished this astonishing feat in July 2003 when he threw an Aerobie Pro flying ring further than anyone has ever thrown any object in the history of measurement.

FELINES 2, HUMANS 0

In 1936, with war looming, entrepreneurs in Portisham, Devon, came up with a brainwave in order to cheer up the population: cat racing. Based on greyhound racing, and with an electric mouse instead of a hare, the sport proved hugely popular, with hundreds flocking to a specially built arena for the races. Unfortunately, the idea was a lot better in theory than it was in reality. When the traps opened, the cats invariably preferred to lie curled up inside, and when they did finally emerge they would end up fighting each other.

Only a few weeks after it opened, Britain's first cat-racing stadium was quietly closed down.

The following year a similar fate befell Britain's first cheetah race, staged at Romford Greyhound Stadium. The prospect of big cats racing each other at speeds of 70mph duly drew a big crowd – unaware that when one cheetah sets off after its prey, the others sit down and have a rest.

EXTREME POGO

As its name suggests, aficionados of Extreme Pogo perform stunts or tricks on a pogo stick. These include pogoing down flights of stairs, along narrow beams, and performing intricate midair acrobatics on specially modified pogo sticks capable of bouncing over 6ft in the air.

GOOGLEWHACKING

Some of the most popular pastimes don't even involve getting out of your chair. Take googlewhacking, for example. A googlewhack is a query consisting of two words entered into the google search engine that returns a single result. As most queries return results in excess of one million, there is more to the pastime than might initially meet the eye.

There are also strict rules governing what does and does not constitute a legitimate googlewhack. These are:

- No quotes or other punctuation in the search terms
- The words must individually appear in an online dictionary such as dictionary.com or answers.com
- The found page must be a real article and not a list of words

As with all sports, there are cheats. Some fans of the craze have gone so far as to create tools that will automatically find googlewhacks. In 2004 comedian Dave Gorman went one stage further by trying to locate ten 'owners' of googlewhacks, from around the globe, in a row.

GEOCACHING

The invention of the Global Positioning System (GPS), which can pinpoint the user's position anywhere on earth using tracker satellites, has been a boon to explorers and the manufacturers of car satellite navigation systems. It has also led to the creation of the new sport of geocaching. Based loosely on the traditional outdoor pursuit of orienteering, geocaching involves the use of GPS receivers to find a 'geocache' (or 'cache') placed anywhere in the world. A typical cache is a small, waterproof container containing a logbook and 'treasure', usually trinkets of little value.

INTERNATIONAL KING OF SPORTS

In the early 1970s *Monty Python* brought the world the 'Upper Class Twit of the Year', a contest in which five particularly dim members of the aristocracy were required to complete a course with such obstacles as jumping over a box of matches and removing the bra of a debutante.

The spirit of this inspired madness lives on today thanks to the International King of Sports competition. This annual event pits contestants from around the world in a series of daft challenges loosely based on recognised athletic events. They include:

- Three metre sprint: The races last under a second and require a photo finish to determine who has won.

- 10G human slalom: Contestants run downhill, taking a zigzag course through ten gates, each composed of a pair of flags on poles.

- Association Bobbage: Contestants wearing flippers jump into a swimming pool from a platform, the height of which is gradually raised. The aim is to land without your head going underwater.

- Backwards 200m: This is a 200m race in which the contestants run backwards.

- Fall down: Contestants have to fall to the floor as fast as possible from a standing position. For a fall to be valid the contestants head must make contact with a cushioned pressure-sensitive pad on the floor.

- Headlong dive: Contestants jump headlong into a sandpit; if their feet touch the sand, their effort is a no-jump.

- International skids: Contestants take a short run-up to a lubricant-coated track, on which they skid. Skids only count if the contestant does not fall over.

- Tennis whack: The contestants hit a tennis ball into the air as high as possible. Whoever's ball takes the longest to return to the ground is the winner.

- Speed-gun run: Contestants sprint down a 20m track; their speed is measured close to the end, just before they run into an upright crash mat.

- Under hurdles: Identical to the 110m hurdles track event, except that the competitors must go under the horizontal bar of the hurdle instead of over it.

ULTIMATE

The object of the game is to score points by passing a flying disc into the end zone of the opposing team, similar to American football. The main stipulation is that players may not run while holding the disc. The game was originally called 'Ultimate Frisbee', until the disc manufacturer Wham-O pointed out that 'Frisbee' is a trademark. Spoilsports.

THE WORLD'S HIGHEST-PAID FOOTBALLERS

1. **Michael Ballack**, Chelsea (£20 million a year)

2. **Ronaldinho**, Barcelona (£15m)

3. **David Beckham**, Real Madrid, (£14m)

4. **Ronaldo**, Real Madrid (£13.3m)

5. **Wayne Rooney**, Manchester United (£11.1m)

3. **Zinedine Zidane**, Real Madrid (£8.8m)

4. **Christian Vieiri**, Internazionale, (£8.2m)

5. **Alessandro Del Piero**, Juventus, (£6.5m)

6. **Frank Lampard**, Chelsea (£6.4m)

7. **Raul**, Real Madrid, (£6.3m)

8. **Thierry Henry**, Arsenal, (£6.3m)

9. **John Terry**, Chelsea, (£5.9m)

10. **Luis Figo**, Real Madrid, (£5.8m)

With these figures seemingly changing as often as footballers girlfriends (and often some players haircuts) this information was accurate at time of publication. Figures are based on estimated annual earnings from wages and commercial endorsements. Data compiled by *France Football magazine*, 2006.

HOWZAT! THE 10 WAYS OF GETTING OUT IN CRICKET

Caught

Bowled

Leg before wicket

Stumped

Handled the ball

Timed out

Double hit

Hit wicket

Run out

Obstructing the field

IT'S A DOG'S LIFE

It is perhaps fitting that the man who gave his name to the world's biggest dog show worked for a dog biscuit manufacturer. In the late nineteenth century Charles Cruft spent his life travelling to dog shows as a salesman, and after a while he realised that such a popular pastime merited a national competition. In 1886 Cruft's first dog show, billed as the 'First Great Terrier Show', had 57 classes and 600 entries. The first show named 'Crufts' – 'Cruft's Greatest Dog Show' – was held at the Royal Agricultural Hall, Islington, in 1891. It was the first at which all breeds were invited to compete, with around 2,000 dogs and almost 2,500 entries.

Today the event is staged over four days at the NEC in Birmingham, with entries restricted to dogs which have won at qualifying competitions across the country. Animals compete to be awarded 'Best of Breed', which allows them to go forward to the next stage, 'Best In Group'. There are seven categories: gun dog, utility, toys, hounds, working, pastoral and terrier. The seven category winners then vie with each other to win the coveted 'Best In Show' award.

HOW TO TELL THE SEX OF A BUDGIE

Keeping and showing budgies is a major international pastime. The British Budgerigar Society was set up in 1925 and now has a membership of more than 3,000. Every year it stages the World Championship, which, as its name suggests, attracts fanciers from as far afield as the USA and Belgium. The society also offers its own tips to bird owners on solving the knotty problem of identifying the sex of their budgie. The secret is to look at the colour of the nose, known as the cere. Healthy, adult female Budgies have a brownish cere. The cere of male budgies is blue.

So now you know.

SNOOKER PLUS

Fearing that the popularity of his sport was in terminal decline, reigning world champion Joe Davis proposed radical changes to the game in a bid to make it more interesting. In 1959 he introduced Snooker Plus, in which a purple ball worth ten points was placed between the brown and blue, and an orange ball worth eight points placed between the blue and pink. The idea was to encourage break-building, as the addition of these two new balls now meant that the maximum possible break increased from 147 to 210.

Snooker Plus was premiered in October 1959 at the *News of the World* tournament, but proved universally unpopular with both players and spectators and was quietly dropped.

Davis should not have worried, however. In 1985 his namesake Steve Davis, along with Dennis Taylor, contested the final of the Embassy World Championship and were watched by a staggering 18.5 million television viewers.

HARD YARDS

The father of the modern marathon is Greek soldier Pheidippides, who in 490BC ran approximately 26 miles between Marathon and Athens in order to break the news to the Athenians that the Persians had been defeated in battle. The fact modern marathons are run over a distance of 26 miles 385 yards is down to more prosaic reasons. At the 1908 Olympic Games in London, Queen Alexandra, consort of Edward VII, ordered that the distance be extended those extra yards so that Princess Mary and her children could watch the start of the race from the nursery window of Windsor Castle. Today, exhausted and embittered runners traditionally shout out 'God Save the Queen' as they stagger beyond the 26-mile mark.

HOW TO PLAY CRAPS

Craps is a game that all fans of American gangster movies have heard of, but few know how to play. In fact, the game is very simple. Each player throws two dice: if they throw 2, 3, or 12 (craps) on their first throw they lose, but win with 7 or 11. If the player's first throw is 4, 5, 6, 8, 9 or 10 this number becomes the *point,* and the player continues until they throw the same number again and win, or throw a 7 and lose. The game was developed from the old English game of hazard, which has similar rules. Hazard is named after the ancient Arabic dice game of Az-Zahr.

POOH STICKS

The game of Pooh Sticks – dropping sticks off a bridge into a river and seeing which one emerges first on the other side – was first mentioned in AA Milne's timeless children's classic *Winnie The Pooh,* and was played by Milne and his son Christopher Robin on a bridge in Ashdown Forest in East Sussex. Somewhat inevitably, the game has been subsequently hijacked by overgrown Pooh enthusiasts and now has its own world championship, staged at Day's Lock at Dorchester-on-Thames in Oxfordshire. Even more predictably, the English are rubbish at it. In 2005 the title was won by a team from the Czech Republic. One team member explained the secret of their success thus: 'We looked for the fastest-flowing part of the river and threw the stick there.'

LESSER-KNOWN OXFORD VERSUS CAMBRIDGE VARSITY MATCHES

The sporting rivalry between Oxford and Cambridge University is thought by most people to be restricted to rowing and rugby. However there are more than twenty sports in which 'Blues' can be awarded. These include: football, basketball, cross country, golf, squash, swimming, yachting, lacrosse, karate and netball.

The sports for which a Half or Discretionary Blue can be awarded are even more diverse, and include: ballroom dancing, boardsailing, chess, cricket, Eton fives, korfball, life saving, real tennis, skiing, tae kwon do and Ultimate Frisbee.

WIFE CARRYING

Who needs marriage counselling when the sport of wife carrying is so much better for marital harmony? Invented as a joke in Finland, the sport does not in fact require the male and female participants to be husband and wife – but it probably helps with the teamwork. Essentially the object is for the man to carry his wife around a devilishly tough obstacle course in the fastest time. Over the years a number of specialist carrying techniques have evolved, including piggyback, fireman's carry, and the most popular Estonian style, in which the wife hangs upside down with her legs over her husband's shoulders.

The popularity of the sport among Finnish men is due to the fact that it is not only a test of strength and endurance, but the winner traditionally gets his wife's weight in beer as a prize.

SUDOKU

Sudoku puzzles have become the craze of the twenty-first century, filling newspapers, books, magazines and even TV programmes. The aim of Sudoku is to fill a 9x9 grid made up of 3x3 subsections (known as regions) so that each row, column and region contains the digits 1-9. The popularity of the puzzle is that while it appears simple, it is in fact extremely difficult. The name '*Sudoku*' is the Japanese abbreviation of a longer phrase, '*Suuji wa dokushin ni kagiru*' (meaning 'the digits must remain single').

CROSSWORD CRAZY

Despite the popularity of modern brain-teasers like Sudoku, crosswords remain the puzzle of choice among aficionados. The first crossword appeared in the *New York World* on 21 December 1913. It was written by Arthur Wynne, a puzzle enthusiast from Liverpool, and described as a 'word-cross' puzzle. Strangely, it was not until 1924 that the first crossword appeared in a British newspaper, the *Sunday Express.*

(Have a go at cracking this crossword, see overleaf on p.110)

FICTITIOUS SPORTS

Anbo-Jitsu: fictitious martial art first shown in an episode of *Star Trek: The Next Generation.* Two armoured opponents each wear a solid visor that renders them blind, then attempt to beat each other senseless with a large staff.

Brockian Ultra-Cricket: Described as 'a curious game which involved suddenly hitting people for no readily apparent reason and then running away', this sport was dreamed up by the late Douglas Adams for his novel *Life, the Universe and Everything.*

Rollerball: a bloodthirsty version of ice hockey played on roller-skates, this sport first appeared in a science-fiction novel by William Harrison, which was later turned into a successful movie starring James Caan.

BASEketball: a zany mixture of baseball and basketball created specifically by comedy writer David Zucker for his 1998 movie of the same name starring Trey Parker and Matt Stone, creators of *South Park.*

Quidditch: invented by author JK Rowling and featured in her *Harry Potter* books, Quidditch is an aerial ball game played by pupils at the Hogwarts school of witchcraft and wizardry.

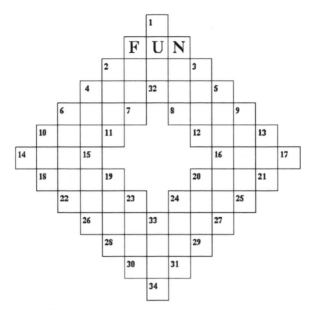

Clues

2-3.	What bargain hunters enjoy.
4-5.	A written acknowledgment.
6-7.	Such and nothing more.
10-11.	A bird.
14-15.	Opposed to less.
18-19.	What this puzzle is.
22-23.	An animal of prey.
26-27.	The close of a day.
28-29.	To elude.
30-31.	The plural of is.
8-9.	To cultivate.
12-13.	A bar of wood or iron.
16-17.	What artists learn to do.
20-21.	Fastened.
24-25.	Found on the seashore.
10-18.	The fibre of the gomuti palm.

6-22.	What we all should be.
4-26.	A day dream.
2-11.	A talon.
19-28.	A pigeon.
F-7.	Part of your head.
23-30.	A river in Russia.
1-32.	To govern.
33-34.	An aromatic plant.
N-8.	A fist.
24-31.	To agree with.
3-12.	Part of a ship.
20-29.	One.
5-27.	Exchanging.
9-25.	To sink in mud.
13-21.	A boy.

The solution to this puzzle can be found at the back of the book on p139.

OBSCURE SPORTING TERMINOLOGY

Ferret: a terrible cricket batsman

Succeeding spot: a marked line the offence must cross in order to achieve a first down in American football

Fisticuffs: a whole section in the laws of ice hockey

Ragging: keeping the puck due to clever stick handling in ice hockey

Floor violation: violating the rules of basketball, but not by preventing an opponent's movement or causing him harm

Swing man: a basketball player who can either play forward or guard

Zamboni: the brand of machine used to clean the ice between periods in ice hockey

Coffin corner: the part of the pitch a punter in American football aims to hit so the opposition can't easily return the ball

Coathanger: a dangerously high tackle in Australian Rules Football

Bunt: a deliberately soft tap with a baseball bat

Ankle-breaker: a basketball move so fast the opposition can't react to it in time

Stutter step: approaching the net with small steps during a rally in tennis

THREE FAMOUS SPORTING TERMS NAMED AFTER REAL PEOPLE

Gaylord: a move on the high bars named after American gymnast Mitch Gaylord. Gaylor's other claim to fame was in 1995, when he appeared as actor Chris O'Donnell's stunt double in the movie *Batman Forever*.

Fosbury Flop: a style of high jump named after American athlete Dick Fosbury. The term was coined by a reporter from a newspaper from Fosbury's native Oregon.

Triple Salchow: a figure skating manoeuvre named after Swedish skater Ulrich Salchow, who won the World Championship a record ten times between 1901 and 1911.

SPORTING DEATHS

Sporting pastimes are, most of the time, hugely beneficial to one's health and wellbeing. However, couch potatoes can argue that the following tragic endings are evidence that sport can, in fact, be deadly.

George Summers: the first man to be killed by a cricket ball when, during a game between Notts and the MCC in 1870, he was struck on the head by a delivery which reared up off a stone on the pitch.

Bing Crosby: in 1977 the veteran US entertainer finished a round of golf in Spain with the words 'Thanks for the game, fellas.' Next moment he dropped dead on the eighteenth green, felled by a massive heart attack.

William of Orange: while out riding in 1702 the king's horse stumbled over a molehill, throwing him to the ground and breaking his collarbone. He subsequently contracted pneumonia and died. Jacobite rebels were heard to toast 'the little gentleman in the black velvet waistcoat'.

Ivan the Terrible: the feared Russian Tsar breathed his last in 1584 while playing chess.

Vladimir Smirnov: during the 1982 World Fencing Championship, Smirnov, representing the Soviet Union, was killed when his opponent's blade snapped and pierced his face mask.

Esteban Domeno: in 1924 Domeno became the first recorded fatality at the Pamplona Bull Run.

Jim Fixx: the man credited with inventing the jogging craze dropped dead of a heart attack in 1984 – while out jogging.

Charles VIII: the French king was walking across a real tennis court in 1498 when he banged his head on a low beam – he lapsed into a terminal coma a few hours later.

Thomas Grice: killed after puncturing his abdomen with his belt buckle during a football match in 1897.

CHASING THE BANKNOTE

Just as ornithologists track the migration of birds by ringing them, so it is possible to follow the circuitous progress of banknotes.

There are now special websites dedicated to tracking money. Users register a bill by entering its serial number, and if someone else has already registered the bill, then the 'route' of the bill can be displayed.

BOOK CROSSING

Book crossing, BC, BCing, or BXing, is the slightly creepy practice of leaving a book in a public place to be picked up and read by others, who then do likewise. The idea is to release books into the 'wild' to be found by other people.

STONE SKIPPING

Have you ever wondered why your stone only skims three times before sinking while others seem capable of skimming their stone for ever? The answer is that they have probably read research by French physicist Lyderic Bocquet into how to skim the perfect stone.

According to Bocquet, an angle of about 20 degrees between the stone and the water's surface is optimal. Changes in speed and rotation do not change this fact.

This, of course, is old news to members of the North American Stone Skipping Association (NASSA), which holds world championships every year in locations from Spain to Scotland.

Member Kurt Steiner currently holds the world record after getting his stone to skip 40 times during a tournament in Pennsylvania in 2002. According to Lyderic Bocquet that would have required a speed of 12 metres per second (25 mph), with a rotation of 14 revolutions per second.

The rules of competitive stone skipping, as set down by NASSA, are:

- The stone's diameter shall not exceed 3in at any point

- The stone must have been formed naturally

- The stone must bounce three times before sinking

- The stone that skims the farthest within the marked lane wins, irrespective of the number of bounces

- Each competitor gets five attempts, with the longest skim counting

MONOPOLY AROUND THE WORLD

Patented by Charles Darrow in 1935, the game of Monopoly has become popular throughout the world. As a result, each country has adapted the board to suit its own locations.

In **Argentina**, the game is known as 'El Estanciero', with streets changed for districts located in different provinces.

Australia originally used the London board, but with dollars instead of pounds. There is now a special Australian Edition with streets from all over the country.

In the **Colombian** version each colour group is a different city, including Bogotá, Medellín and Cali.

In keeping with the growth of the European Union, **Europe Special Edition** has been launched. Instead of streets, it uses the names of capital cities of countries that are already members of the European Union, and some which are expected to be. Currency, of course, is in Euros.

The **German** version uses streets and districts from Cologne and Munich.

In **Iran** Tehran is used, although certain versions use pre-Revolution street names.

Dublin is the featured city in **Ireland**, although there are two versions featuring the Irish pound and Euro.

Both Japanese and American English boards are sold in **Japan**. The Japanese board includes districts from several major Japanese cities: the most expensive property is Tokyo's Ginza district, followed by Osaka's Umeda.

There are two versions in **South Africa**. The 1963 apartheid version features Durban, Bloemfontein, Cape Town, Johannesburg; the more up-to-date 2002 version KwaZulu-Natal, South-Eastern Cape Region, Garden Route Region, Johannesburg and Western Cape Region.

Spain has Madrid, Barcelona, Bilbao and Valencia editions. The 70th anniversary edition includes the capital cities of the autonomous communities instead of streets. There is also an edition based on the Spanish national football team.

In **Venezuela** 'Monopolio' features streets and properties from the city of Caracas, and the currency is bolívares.

In **Malaysia**, there is an independent version of Monopoly known as Saidina, featuring local places and currency, and written in the local language of Bahasa Melayu.

THE WORLD'S MOST POPULAR GAMES

According to the About Board Games and Card Games website, the ten most popular games in terms of user inquiries are:

1. Monopoly: buying and selling property to amass a fortune and avoid bankruptcy

2. Risk/Risk 2210 AD: world-domination game with a newer version introducing space and underwater exploration.

3. Mah Jongg: tile-based strategy game invented in China

4. Scrabble: making words from random tiles in order to gain points

5. Beyblades: fighting, spinning tops from Japan

6 Backgammon: ancient dice game of skill and chance

7. Battleships: two players deploy their fleets and try to destroy their opponent's by predicting on which square they are positioned

8. Stratego: war-based strategy game

9. Draughts: also known as checkers, this board game dates back to the sixteenth century

10 Chess: the king of board games, played with scientific precision by its greatest exponents

BATTLE OF THE CHESS COMPUTERS

The first chess computers were basic indeed. The Fidelity CC1 had just one level of play, would allow you to make illegal moves, and would only play with the black pieces.

Time and technology has moved on, however, and in 2004 two chess supercomputers – Hydra and Shredder 8 – battled it out to see which was the greatest.

Although Shredder 8 was a multiple-times world computer chess champion it was defeated 5.5–2.5, winning three games and drawing the rest. In an informal match at the same tournament, Hydra took on International Grandmaster Evgeny Vladimirov of Kazakhstan, and defeated him by a score of 3.5–0.5.

BINGO CALLS

1. Kelly's Eye

2. One little duck

3. You and me

4. Knock at the door

5. Man alive

6. Tom's tricks

7. Lucky

8. Garden gate

9. Doctor's orders

10. Tony's den

11. Legs

12. One dozen

13. Unlucky for some

14. Valentine's day

15. Young and keen

16. Sweet

17. Dancing queen

18. 23.061 mmComing of age

19. Goodbye teens

20. One score

21. Key to the door

22. Two little ducks

23. Thee and me

24. Two dozen

25. Duck and dive

26. Pick and mix

27. Stairs to heaven

28. Overweight

29. Rise and shine

30. Dirty Gertie

31. Get up and run

32. Buckle my shoe

BINGO CALLS (continued . . .)

33. Dirty knees
34. Ask for more
35. Jump and jive
36. Three dozen
37. More than eleven
38. Christmas cake
39. Steps
40. Naughty
41. Life's begun
42. Winnie the Pooh
43. Down on your knees
44. All the fours
45. Halfway there
46. Up to tricks
47. Four and seven
48. Four dozen
49. PC
50. Half a century
51. Tweak of the thumb
52. Danny La Rue
53. Stuck in the tree
54. Clean the door
55. Snakes alive
56. Was she worth it
57. Heinz varieties
58. Make them wait
59. Brighton line
60. Five dozen
61. Baker's bun

BINGO CALLS (continued . . .)

62. Turn the screw

63. Tickle me

64. Red raw

65. Old age pension

66. Clickety click

67. Made in heaven

68. Saving grace

69. Either way up

70. Blind

71. Bang the drum

72. Six dozen

73. Queen Bee

74. Candy stripe

75. Strive and strive

76. Trombones

77. Sunset Strip

78. Heaven's gate

79. One more time

80. Eight and blank

81. Stop and run

82. Straight on through

83. Time for tea

84. Seven dozen

85. Staying alive

86. Between the sticks

87. Torquay and Devon

88. Two fat ladies

89. Nearly there

90. Top of the shop

A QUICK ROUND OF DARTS TERMINOLOGY

Annie's room: number 1
Upstairs: the numbers on the top half of the board
Bucket of nails: three 1s
Middle for diddle: throwing for bullseye for the right to start the game
Lord Nelson: a score of 111
Shanghai: scoring a number, its double and its treble with three darts
Three in a bed: three darts in the same number
Ton: 100
Ton eighty: 180
Right church, wrong pew: a double of the wrong number
Bed and breakfast: 26 made up of 5, 20 and 1
Bag of nuts: a score of 45

HOW TO DRINK A YARD OF ALE

Usually found on the wall behind the bar, a yard of ale is a 3ft glass vessel with a bulb on the bottom designed to hold around three pints of beer. The earliest reference to this type of glass was recorded in the diary of a John Evelyn in 1685. He referred to the Sheriff and the Commander of the Kentish Troop in Bromley drinking to the health of King James II from a 'glasse of a yard long'.

The story goes that the glass was specifically designed to meet the needs of stagecoach drivers, who were always in a hurry to get to their destinations. The glass had to be long enough to hand to the driver without his having to leave the stagecoach. The design of the glass meant that the stagecoach driver could drive without losing control and drink at the same time. He could also have his glass refilled without letting go of the reins.

The secret of drinking, or sculling, from a yard of ale is, according to experts, to gently rotate the glass while it is positioned at the lips, thereby preventing the beer from spilling out at the sides.

Interestingly, former Australian prime minister Bob Hawke once held the world record for sculling a yard of ale.

SOME FAMOUS QUOTES ABOUT DRINKING

Drinking is inextricably linked with sport, and indeed many sporting pastimes owe their existence to the joys of pub camaraderie and the invention of games to pass the time during drinking sessions. Here are just a few memorable quotes about drink:

'You can't be a real country unless you have a beer and an airline – it helps if you have some kind of a football team, or some nuclear weapons, but at the very least you need a beer.'
– Frank Zappa

'Always do sober what you said you'd do drunk. That will teach you to keep your mouth shut.'
– Ernest Hemingway

'He was a wise man who invented beer.'
– Plato

'Work is the curse of the drinking classes.'
– Oscar Wilde

'Beer is proof that God loves us and wants us to be happy.'
– Benjamin Franklin

'Without question, the greatest invention in the history of mankind is beer. Oh, I grant you that the wheel was also a fine invention, but the wheel does not go nearly as well with pizza.'
– Dave Barry

'Give me a woman who loves beer and I will conquer the world.'
– Kaiser Wilhelm

'I drink to make other people interesting.'
– George Jean Nathan

THE ANGLER'S CALENDAR (c.1493)

The *salmon* in April and May, and a little while after it is at its very best and the salmon remains so till the end of St James. Then it must be left to St Andrew's Day and it is best between St Michael's Day and St Martin's.

The *pike* is best in July, only the pike is good at all times, only excepted when he sees the rye he has spawned.

The forepart of the *pike* or *carp* is better always than the hind part. It is the same with other fishes.

A *tench* is always best in June.

The *perch* is always good except in May or April.

The *bream* or *mackerel* are good in February and March.

The *mullet* is good in March or April.

A *kullunck* is best at Candlemas Day and continues good in April.

The *rudd* is good in February and March and falls off in May.

The *gudgeons* are good in February, March and April, till May. Only the young gudgeon is always good with parsley.

A *bleak* is best in Autumn.

The *sticklebacks* are good in March, and in the beginning of May. When they are full they shall be stirred with eggs.

The *eel* is good in May till the day of the Assumption of Our Lady.

A *lamphern*, the brother of the lamprey, is good from the thirteenth Mass to the day of Our Lady's Annunciation.

The *crayfish* is best in March and April and particularly when the moon increases, then they are so much the better.

INTERNATIONAL PLAYING CARD PACKS

Country	Standard Deck	Suits
UK	52	Diamonds, Hearts, Clubs, Spades
Germany	36	Leaves, Acorns, Hearts, Bells
Italy	40	Swords, Batons, Cups, Coins
Switzerland	32	Shields, Acorns, Flowers, Bells
Spain	40	Swords, Clubs, Cups, Coins

MARATHON MADNESS

Most of us would quake at the prospect of running 26 miles. But compared to some long-distance endurance races, the marathon is little more than a warm-up. Some of the toughest include:

Marathon des Sables: 151 miles in 6 days across the Sahara desert

South Pole Ultra-marathon: 45km to the South Pole – in snow shoes

Cornbelt Run: a 24-hour continuous run around a 400m track

Self-transcendence Race: the longest foot race in the world – over 3,100 miles

Spartathlon: 246km from Athens to Sparta

Jungle Run: 200km over 7 days through the Amazon jungle

SPOOFED

Pub games are as varied as the types of beer on sale in them, but one of the most popular – especially after a few drinks have been consumed – is Spoof. Normally played by five people, each person takes five coins. They must then secrete between one and five in their fist, which is then placed on the table in front of them. Each player must then guess how many coins are being held in total without duplicating another person's guess. When everyone has had their turn the coins are revealed and the person who guessed correctly drops out. The game continues until there is only one player left. This is the loser, and their punishment usually involves getting the next round in.

SOME CLASSIC ARCADE GAMES

PACMAN: Inspired, according to its Japanese designers, by a pizza with a slice missing, this little yellow blob must make its way around a maze while eating energy pills, while at the same time avoiding a series of multi-coloured ghosts.

SPACE INVADERS: The all-time classic. You control a moving gun emplacement and must pick off the slowly-descending rows of aliens before they land on earth.

FROGGER: The task is to get a frog from the bottom of the screen to the top, avoiding a series of increasingly difficult obstacles.

SIMON: Devilishly simple and addictive, players must follow the exact sequence of Simon's flashing lights.

DONKEY KONG: Evil gorilla Donkey Kong has stolen Mario's girlfriend. Can he get her back? The original 'platform' game, which introduced the world to SuperMario. Donkey Kong got his name because the Japanese designers thought 'Donkey' meant 'stubborn'.

TETRIS: Descending bricks must be quickly organised into a solid whole.

ASTEROIDS: You are the captain of a spaceship caught in the middle of an asteroid field. Can you blast the asteroids before they blast you?

SOME RANDOM FACTS ABOUT THE NATIONAL LOTTERY

The National Lottery is a national pastime, with millions of people attempting to scoop the jackpot despite odds of over 14,000,000–1. Here are some random facts about the national obsession:

- The first national lottery in Britain was run in 1569
- The first ever National Lottery draw took place on Saturday 19 November 1994
- Total ticket sales are over £55 billion to the end of February 2006
- By March 2006 over £18.3 billion had been raised by the Lottery for the good causes and 232,000 grants had been made.
- More than half of all the Lottery grants made have been grants of less than £5000 – bringing benefits to communities across the United Kingdom.
- A survey revealed two of the most popular places for jackpot winners to keep their tickets are 'in their Bibles' and 'in their underwear'.

TUG OF WAR: THE SPECIFICATIONS

According to the Tug of War International Federation, the rope used in competition must be no less than 10cm or more than 12.5cm in circumference, and must be free from knots or other holdings for the hands. The ends of the rope shall have a whipping finish. The minimum length of the rope must not be less than 33.5m.

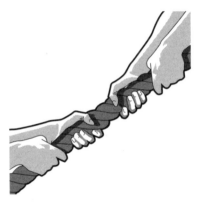

GROUSE SHOOTING

An estimated 350,000 grouse are shot every year. The grouse-shooting season runs from August 12th until mid-December. Before this, the grouse live a semi-natural life, breeding and living out on the moors but in a 'managed' environment. Up to 35 million pheasants are intensively reared each year in purpose-built hatcheries, cages and pens.

Other birds hunted as game include: Blackcock, capercailzie, snipe, golden plover, jacksnipe, lapwing, partridge, pheasant, ptarmigan, quail, widgeon, wild duck.

SPORTING INSULTS

'Footballers are scum ... if they weren't football players, most of them would be in prison, it's as simple as that.'
– Alan Sugar, former Tottenham Hotspur chairman

A WORD OF ADVICE TO GOLFERS

'If you drink, don't drive. Don't even putt.'
– Dean Martin

WOMEN'S FOOTBALL

Although there are records of the game being played by women as early as the 1890s, it was not until 1969 that the Women's Football Association was formed in England. Typically, the Football Association took a dim view of the women's game and banned them from playing on members' grounds. However, such was the groundswell of interest in the women's game, in 1971 the FA relented. In the same year UEFA recommended that the women's game should be taken under the control of the national associations in each country.

In the 1970s, Italy became the first country with professional women football players, albeit on a part-time basis. The first full-time professional team was the United States national squad, and in 1992 Japan was the first country to have a professional women's football league.

Women's football came of age in 1991 with its first World Cup, won by the USA – a country where the women's game has taken off massively compared to the men's game.

STAYING POWER

When Feroze Khan died in Pakistan at the age of 101 in 2005 a little piece of Olympic history died with him. At the time of his death Khan was the world's oldest Olympic medal winner, part of the Indian hockey team which won silver at the 1928 Games in Holland. 'This is ample proof of the fact that discipline and individuals with sporting habits can live longer,' Khan said on his 100 birthday. The previous oldest medal winner was James Rockefeller of the USA who died in 2004. Rockefeller won a gold medal in rowing in the 1924 Paris Olympics.

THE SPEAR TACKLE

A spear tackle in rugby union and rugby league is where a player is picked up by an opponent on their side, and turned so that they are upside down. The opponent then drops the player on the ground, often head or neck first. It is highly dangerous and can cause serious injury. The most famous example of this tackle occurred in the first Test between the British Lions and New Zealand in 2005 when Lions skipper Brian O'Driscoll was spear tackled by Tama Umaga and Keven Mealamu and was forced out of the tour after just five minutes.

COLEMANBALLS

A favourite pastime of the armchair sports fan is spotting Colemanballs – that is the inadvertent gaffes made by commentators and sportsmen which are celebrated in the satirical magazine *Private Eye* and named after the arch exponent of such gaffes, BBC commentator David Coleman. Some of the classics reported over the years include:

'This is really a lovely horse, I once rode her mother.'
–Ted Walsh

'Moses Kiptanui – the 19 year old Kenyan, who turned 20 a few weeks ago'
– David Coleman

'We now have exactly the same situation as we had at the start of the race, only exactly the opposite'
– Murray Walker

'Hodge scored for Forest after 22 seconds – totally against the run of play'
– Peter Lorenzo

'We actually got the winner three minutes from the end but then they equalized'
– Ian McNail

'The lead car is absolutely unique, except for the one behind it which is identical'
– Murray Walker

'I owe a lot to my parents, especially my mother and father'
– Greg Norman

'Sure there have been injuries and deaths in boxing – but none of them serious'
– Alan Minter

'The racecourse is as level as a billiard ball'
– John Francombe

'I never comment on referees and I'm not going to break the habit of a lifetime for that prat'
–Ron Atkinson

COLEMANBALLS (CONTINUED . . .)

'Ah, isn't that nice, the wife of the Cambridge president is kissing the cox of the Oxford crew.'
–Harry Carpenter, BBC TV Boat Race 1977

'Here we are in the Holy Land of Israel – a Mecca for tourists.'
–David Vine

'Morcelli has four fastest 1500-metre times ever. And all those times are at 1500 metres.'
–David Coleman

'To play Holland, you have to play the Dutch.'
–Ruud Gullit

'Well, either side could win it, or it could be a draw.'
–Ron Atkinson

'For those of you watching in black and white, Spurs are in the all-yellow strip.'
–John Motson

'There goes Juantorena down the back straight, opening his legs and showing his class'
–Ron Pickering at the Montreal Olympics

'One of the reasons Arnie [Arnold Palmer] is playing so well is that, before each tee-shot, his wife takes out his balls and kisses them – Oh my God, what have I just said?'
– USTV commentator

HOUSE OF COMMONS FOOTBALL TEAM

When they are not busy debating the important issues of the day, members of the House of Commons like nothing better than donning their boots and taking on all-comers at football. In the past the cross-party team have played sides from other governments, the media and even all-star elevens made up of retired professional footballers.

RON MANAGER

One of the most popular character in BBC's *Fast Show* was Ron Manager. Ron, played by Paul Whitehouse, was a football pundit whose mostly irrelevant contributions concerned misty-eyed recollections of 'small boys in the park' and 'jumpers for goalposts.' Although Whitehouse always denied that Ron was based on anybody real, in his autobiography *Blessed*, George Best claims that he was told by Paul Whitehouse that the late Fulham manager Alec Stock was the inspiration. Best described Stock as a 'lovely bubbly character who had a romantic attitude about how football should be played' and as a manager 'whose teams always played with style'.

GAMES FOR GEEKS

The Cyberathlete Professional League (CPL) was founded in 1997 as a professional sports tournament for computer gamers. The CPL holds tournaments throughout the USA, Europe, Latin America and Asia, and has hosted a variety of teams and players usually regarded as the best in their respective games. The CPL's aim is to make computer gaming a viable competitive and spectator event, on the level of athletic sports. However it remains debatable whether expertise at games like Doom, Alien vs Predator 2, Halo, Quake and Doom is a sign of athletic prowess or of spending too much time locked in a bedroom in front of an X-Box.

GEOFF THOMAS

Geoff Thomas was an accomplished footballer for Crystal Palace and England who was diagnosed with leukaemia in 2003 and given just three years to live. Inspired by the remarkable story of cyclist Lance Armstrong, who was given just a 10 per cent chance of surviving cancer but came back to win seven Tours de France, Thomas set about raising money for cancer research by embarking on his own cycling odyssey. In 2005, Thomas – despite suffering the debilitating effects of chemotherapy – set off to complete the gruelling 2,000-mile route of the Tour, often cycling in excess of 100 miles a day. Remarkably, he not only achieved the feat but in 2006 announced that he was going to take part in the equally challenging Trans America cycle race.

SLEDGING

In cricket, sledging is when the bowler and fielders exchange a few choice words with the batsman in an effort to put them off. Although officially frowned upon as not being in the spirit of the game, it has led to some hilarious banter in the square.

Australian Merv Hughes to Englishman Robin Smith: 'Does your husband play cricket as well?'

Javed Miandad of India called Merv Hughes a fat bus conductor. Hughes then dismissed Miandad and called out 'Tickets Please'.

Malcolm Marshall of the West Indies to David Boon of Australia: 'Now David, are you going to get out now or am I going to have to bowl around the wicket and kill you?'

Shane Warne of Australia wondered out loud how he was going to draw Pakistan's Arjuna Ranatunga out of his crease. Wicketkeeper Ian Healy piped up: 'Put a Mars Bar on a good length. That should do it.'

Australia's Glenn McGrath to Zimbabwe's Eddo Brandes: 'Oi, Brandes, why are you so ****** fat?'
Brandes: 'Cos every time I **** your wife she gives me a biscuit!'

Shane Warne to Daryll Cullinan of South Africa: 'I've been waiting two years to humiliate you again.'
Cullinan: 'Looks like you spent the time eating.'

CALORIES BURNED IN 20 MINUTES

Leisurely walk: 80

Dancing: 120

Cycling: 160

Running: 90

Aerobics: 140

Weights: 140

Cleaning: 50

Driving: 35

Swimming: 100

Tennis: 120

Rowing: 200

Golf: 45

Circuit training: 260

Skipping: 100

Gardening: 160

Skiing: 130

Sex: between 10–50 (depending on vigorousness and effort. Obviously.)

LA TOMATINA

A word of advice: don't go to the Spanish village of Bunol on the last Wednesday in August. On that day the entire village celebrates the end of the tomato season with 'La Tomatina' – in which for more than two hours more than 90,000lb of tomatoes are thrown at everyone and anything in range. This curious practice is thought to have originated in the 1940s when a group of tomato pickers got overexcited after a long lunch.

AN EXPLOSIVE SPORT

The Colombian sport of Tejo is played like quoits, with players tossing a ball, disc or stone into the scoring zone. This, however, is where the similarity ends because instead of aiming for pegs or jacks the object is to hit explosive caps planted in the ground. The player who causes the most explosions is deemed to be the winner.

KNOW YOUR HORSES

Colt: male aged four and under, not castrated and not mated with a mare

Dam: a horse's mother

Gelding: a castrated male

Stallion: males that mates with female horses

Sire: a horse's father

Juvenile: a two-year-old flat racer or a three-to four-year-old jumper

Filly: female up to the age of four

Mare: female four or older or any female that has been bred

Maiden: a horse yet to win a race

FOOTY ON THE AIRWAVES

The 2006 FA Cup final between West Ham and Liverpool was watched by an estimated global audience of 484 million – testament to the fact that watching the Cup final on telly has become a pastime all of its own.

Before TV, however, radio was the only means of keeping in touch with the big match unless you were lucky enough to have a ticket. The first final on radio was Bolton Wanderers versus Manchester City in 1926, although it was only relayed to public halls in Bolton and Manchester. In the following season Cardiff City famously overcame Arsenal 1–0 to take the Cup out of England, and for the first time the match was broadcast in its entirety by the BBC.

The first fully televised final was Preston North End versus Huddersfield in 1938. A TV audience of just 10,000 saw George Mutch convert a penalty in the last minute of extra time to win the Cup for the Lancashire side.

SOUND ADVICE FOR SHOOTERS

If a sportsman true you'd be, listen carefully to me:

Never, never let your gun
Pointed be at anyone;
That it may be unloaded be
Matters not the least to me.

When a hedge or fence you cross
Though of time it cause a loss,
From your gun the cartridge take,
For the greater safety's sake.

If twixt you and neighbouring gun,
Birds may fly or beasts may run,
Let this maxim e'er be thine:
Follow not across the line.

Stops and beaters oft unseen
Lurk behind some leafy screen;
Calm and steady always be:
Never shoot where you can't see.

Keep your place and silent be:
Game can hear and game can see;
Don't be greedy, better spared
Is a pheasant than one shared.

You may kill or you may miss;
But at all times think of this:
All the pheasants ever bred
Won't repay for one man dead.

– Mark Hanbury Beaufoy MP (1854–1922)

THE CYCLING CALENDAR

Professional cyclists know that spring has sprung when the Milan–San Remo race arrives in mid-March. This is the first of the so-called Spring Classics, which kick off the cycling season and lead into the Grand Tours of Italy, France and Spain. The yearly calendar looks like this:

March
Milan–San Remo (Italy)*
Omloop 'Het Volk' (Belgium)

April
Tour of Flanders (Belgium)*
Paris–Roubaix (France)*
Ghent–Wevelgem (Belgium)
Amstel Gold Race (Holland)
La Fleche Wallonne (Belgium)
Liege–Bastogne–Liege (Belgium)*

May
Giro d'Italia (Italy)**

July
Tour de France (France)**

September
Vuelta a Espana (Spain)**

October

Tour of Lombardy *
* These one-day races are known as the 'Monuments' of cycling. Only three riders have ever won all five, and all three were Belgian. They were: Roger De Vlaeminck, Rik Van Looy and Eddy Merckx. One of the Monuments no longer run is the gruelling Bordeaux–Paris race, which was 560km long and partly motor-paced.
** These are the Grand Tours, three-week stage races regarded as the ultimate in the sport. No cyclist has ever won all three Tours in the same year, and only Eddy Merckx, Felice Gimondi, Jacques Anquetil and Bernard Hinault have won all three. America's Lance Armstrong has won the Tour de France a record seven times, ahead of Merckx, Hinault, Anquetil and Miguel Indurain, who have all won it five times.

THE CRICKETER'S BIBLE

Wisden Cricketers' Almanack (often referred to simply as *Wisden* or colloquially as 'the Bible of Cricket') is by far the best-known reference book concerned with the sport of cricket and probably the most famous reference book about any sport published in the world. It was founded in 1864 by the English cricketer John Wisden (1826–1884), and its annual publication has continued uninterrupted to the present day, making it the longest running sports annual in history. It has had only 15 editors in over 140 years, including John Wisden himself for 20 editions (1864 to 1884), Sydney Pardon for 35 editions (1891 to 1925), and Norman Preston for 28 editions (1952 to 1980). Matthew Engel is the current editor.

GOAL CELEBRATIONS

In the old days, a goal would be celebrated with a firm handshake and a 'well done, old boy'. Now, however, no striker worth his salt takes to the field without a choreographed goal celebration ready for the moment when he hits the back of the net. Some of the most famous celebrations include:

Roger Milla (Cameroon): Boogying with the corner flag
Alan Shearer (Newcastle United): left arm raised in salute
Faustino Asprilla (Newcastle United): cartwheels
Robbie Keane (Tottenham): cartwheel and forward roll followed by pretending to shoot a pistol
Peter Beagrie (Everton): back flip
Mick Channon (Southampton): single windmilling arm
Stuart Pearson (Manchester United): clenched fist raised to the mouth
Denis Law (Manchester United): one arm raised, fingers clutching the cuff of the shirt
Eric Cantona (Manchester United): hands on hips, staring imperiously at the crowd
Jurgen Klinsmann (Tottenham): swallow dive onto the turf
Robbie Fowler (Liverpool): pretending to snort cocaine from the touchline, also lifting his shirt to reveal a slogan in support of the striking Liverpool dockers
Brandi Chastain (USA women's team): removing her shirt to reveal a sports bra
Peter Crouch (England): 'The Crouch' – a play on the 1980s dance-floor move 'The Robot'

'THE TRY'

Rugby union was founded on the amateur ethos and, for over a century, until it finally went professional in 1995, the Barbarians personified this Corinthian ideal. Drawn from players from different clubs and always featuring one uncapped player, the Baa-Baas, as they were known, would traditionally make up the opposition for the final match of a visiting country's tour. Usually lack of cohesion and training, allied with a skinful of beer the night before, meant that they would lose. However in 1973, the Barbarians side to face the New Zealand All Blacks at Cardiff Arms Park was made up largely of the historic 1972 British Lions team that had become the first to win a series in New Zealand.

The match was a classic – cut and thrust, attack and counter-attack by two brilliant teams playing out of their skins. The Baa-Baas won 23-11, but it is their opening try by Gareth Edwards after just four minutes which is still talked about more than thirty years later and will forever be remembered simply as 'The Try'.

Following a kick by New Zealand's Bryan Williams, Phil Bennett launched an audacious counter-attack from in front of his own posts. The ball passed through five pairs of Barbarian hands before scrum half Edwards, steaming onto the ball 40 yards out, dived over for a brilliant score. For many people the commentary by Cliff Morgan – himself a former British Lion – is as much a part of 'The Try' as what happened on the pitch.

'Kirkpatrick to Williams. This is great stuff. Phil Bennett covering, chased by Alistair Scown. Brilliant! Oh, that's brilliant! John Williams. Pullin. John Dawes, great dummy. To David, Tom David, the half-way line. Brilliant by Quinnell. This is Gareth Edwards. A dramatic start! What a score!'

GEORGE BEST'S CLUBS

Although the late George Best is remembered, rightly, for his career at Manchester United, the mercurial and troubled Irishman continued playing on and off for almost a decade after his supposed retirement from the game in 1974 at the age of 27. The table overleaf shows all Bestie's clubs:

GEORGE BEST'S CLUBS (CONTINUED . . .)

Year	Club	Appearances	Goals
1963–74	Manchester United	361	138
1975	Stockport County	3	2
1975–76	Cork Celtic	3	0
1976–78	Los Angeles Aztecs 0	61	29
1976–77	Fulham	47	10
1979–80	Hibernian	22	3
1979–81	San Jose Earthquakes *	86	34
1983	Bournemouth	5	0
1983	Brisbane Lions	4	0

*US teams who played in the equivalent of the British close season.

Between 1966 and 1971 Best played 37 times for Northern Ireland, scoring nine goals. Sadly, due to the team's inability to qualify, one of the greatest players ever produced in the British Isles never played in a World Cup finals.

THE 10 FUNNIEST SPORTS SHOWS
(as nominated by *Observer Sports Monthly*)

1 *Fred Trueman's Indoor League*, Yorkshire TV, 1973–78
Fronted by former Yorkshire and England cricketer Fred Trueman, this featured overweight men playing each other at darts, arm wrestling, shove ha'penny and skittles. Trueman himself got into the non-athletic spirit of proceedings by introducing the show with a pipe in one hand and a pint of bitter in the other. His closing words – 'I'll si' thee' – have become the stuff of legend.

2 *Mike Reid's Under Par*, Discovery Home and Leisure, 2003
This short-lived golf show featured bassoon-voiced Reid, a comedian who had become a national star on *EastEnders,* playing various courses around the country with a style that could only be described as 28-handicap.

3 *Superstars*, BBC 1974–85
Although it has made a return to British screens, aficionados of *Superstars* will always point to its original incarnation as its heyday. Highlights included Kevin Keegan falling off his bike, a drunken Stan Bowles shooting himself in the foot and Brian Jacks beating everybody at squat thrusts.

4 *Salmon Run with Jack Charlton* , BBC, 1994
Jack Charlton won a World Cup winner's medal for England, but won no prizes for this dreadful show based on the popular sport of angling.

5 *Junior Kick Start,* BBC, 1982–92
Fronted by ex-*Blue Peter* stalwart, Peter Purves, *Junior Kick Start* featured youngsters on trial bikes attempting to get round a muddy course in the quickest time. Most viewers watched the show on the off-chance of seeing the contestants come a cropper. Fortunately, this happened on a regular basis.

6 *World of Sport,* ITV, 1965–85
The poor relation to BBC's *Grandstand*, *World of Sport* made up for what it lacked in quality sport with enthusiasm. And enthusiasm was definitely the order of the day when you had to fill an afternoon with wrestling from Preston Town Hall and the World Bus-Jump Classic where men in double-decker buses tried to leap over 100 motorbikes.

7 *World's Strongest Woman,* BBC, 2002
Mindful of their equal opportunities responsibilities, the BBC briefly ditched coverage of *The World's Strongest Man* in favour of its female equivalent. The inaugural contest was held on the Zambezi, near Victoria Falls. Eight contestants battled it out for the coveted Butlin's Trophy, but the show was not strong enough to warrant a second series.

8 *We are the Champions*, BBC, 1975–95
Essentially this was a television version of school sports day. Three teams of kids competed both on the playing field and the swimming pool before being invited by host Ron Pickering to jump into the pool at the same time.

9 *Ski Sunday*, BBC, 1978–
Given that the only British interest in downhill skiing was commentator David Vine, it is amazing that *Ski Sunday* not only survived a first series, but continues to this day.

10 *Kabaddi*, Channel4 , 1991–92
Desperately searching for more sports to add to its portfolio, Channel 4 turned its attentions to the ancient Indian discipline kabaddi. Although hugely popular on the subcontinent, British fixtures such as West Bengal Police versus the Punjab, failed to capture the imagination of the British viewers.

GOLDEN BOOT WINNERS

The scorer of the most goals in a World Cup tournament is awarded the coveted Golden Boot. The winners since 1930 have been:

1930: Guilermo Stabile (Argentina), 8

1934: Oldrich Nejedly (Czechoslovakia), 5

1938: Leonidas (Brazil), 8

1950: Ademir (Brazil), 9

1954: Sandor Kocsis (Hungary), 11

1958: Juste Fontaine (France), 13

1962: Garrincha (Brazil), Valentin Ivanov (Soviet Union), Leonel Sanchez (Chile), Florian Albert (Hungary), Vava (Brazil), Drazan Jerkovic (Yugoslavia), 4

1966: Eusebio (Portugal), 9

1970: Gerd Muller (Germany), 10

1974: Gzegorz Lato (Poland), 7

1978: Mario Kempes (Argentina), 6

1982: Paulo Rossi (Italy), 6

1986: Gary Lineker (England), 6

1990: Salvatore Schillaci (Italy), 6

1994: Hristo Stoichkov (Bulgaria), Oleg Salenko (Russia), 6

1998: Davor Suker (Crotia), 6

2002: Ronaldo (Brazil), 8

2006: Miroslav Klose (Germany), 5

SOLUTION TO THE 1ST EVER CROSSWORD PUZZLE (FROM PAGE 104)

How well did you do?

```
                R
            F   U   N
        S   A   L   E   S
            R   E   C   E   I   P   T
        M   E   R   E       F   A   R   M
    D   O   V   E               R   A   I   L
M   O   R   E                       D   R   A   W
    H   A   R   D               T   I   E   D
        L   I   O   N       S   A   N   D
            E   V   E   N   I   N   G
                E   V   A   D   E
                    A   R   E
                    D
```

Are you now inspired to invent your own extraordinary pastime? Why dont you have a go . . .

If Beer Mat flipping can become one of the greatest pastimes ever, then surely it must be easy to come up with an even better idea . . .

Good luck!

NOTES

INDEX